Rock The SAT Math Test

Rock The SAT Math Test

Published by Exam Masters Tutoring Service, a division of Ontario Inc.
17 Winnifred Avenue
Toronto, ON M4M 2X2

Acknowledgements

This SAT practice test book is the culmination of years of tutoring Grade 11 and 12 high school students for the SAT, ACT, and all high school math subjects. Many thanks to all the students with whom I discussed the subject matter with for their valuable suggestions and corrections to the early versions. I am indebted to the many students past and present that I have personally tutored through Exam Masters Tutoring Service, for challenging me to be the best I can be. Thank you also to our team of mathematicians and math content creation specialists, for their great contribution to this book: Dr. Saravanan Thiyagarajan (PhD in Mathematics), Aleksandar Stevanovic (Certified Math Teacher), and Bryan Ibanez (Bachelor of Mathematics).

Authors Note

This book is primarily created to give students a realistic experience for the SAT Math test. There are 6 full math practice tests, which are organized as section 3 and section 4 for each test. This is to simulate the real test. Each test contains the most commonly tested concepts based on our analysis of the released College Board tests, as well as, concepts that we feel have the potential to be tested.

We really spent a lot of time going over every question to make sure that it would help you prepare well for this test and made sure that there were many questions on the most commonly tested concepts. There are a few questions which may seem really difficult, but for the student who aims for an 800, these types of questions should be expected. For example, most students learn linear geometry, but have never come across the scenario of how to find the shortest distance between a point and a perpendicular line. Concepts like this have the potential to be tested, so we made sure to include them in our tests. We also delved into rarely tested concepts, such as in statistics, and created questions that will really test the students' grasp of statistical concepts. For example, every student has heard of the quartile, but few have heard of the decile.

So, use these tests to their maximum potential and use this book along with a good review source to rock the SAT math test.

Best wishes in your studies,
Exam Masters[TS]

Table of Contents

Rock The SAT Math Test

About the Math Test

In this introductory chapter, we break down the whole SAT math test and show you what it's composed of, what it tests, and how to ace to it. The first thing to realize is that the SAT math test has changed its focus to mainly test students on algebra and problem-solving using real-world scenarios. The majority of it covers Basic Algebra and Advanced Algebra. Therefore, most of the concepts in these two divisions of math are fair game. And there are a lot of concepts. But, the good news is that you've already learned all or most of these concepts in school. The new SAT has really become aligned to your school curriculum. It basically covers most of Grade 11 Math and a tiny bit of Grade 12 Math. Here are the main sections on the SAT math test:

Math Topic	Main Focus	# of Questions	% of Total
Heart of Algebra	mastery of linear equations and systems	19 Questions	32.76 %
Problem Solving and Data Analysis	being quantitatively literate	17 Questions	29.31 %
Passport to Advanced Math	manipulation of complex equations	16 Questions	27.59 %
Additional Topics	understanding of rarer math concepts	6 Questions	10.34 %

From this table, we can see that the additional topics only make up for 10.34% and the rest of the topics account for 89.66% of the total questions in the math section. This is very key for us to know, as it will guide our strategy for the math section (which we will discuss later).

Calculator and No-Calculator Portions

The math test will be Section 3 and Section 4 of the whole SAT and will consist of portions where you will be allowed to use a calculator and portions where you will NOT be allowed to use a calculator. Don't let this scare you, as most of the questions will be solvable without calculators. The calculator will mainly be for questions which give you ugly numbers with decimal places or things like the quadratic formula. In general though, the questions in the no-calculator portion will be solvable faster than the questions in the calculator portions.

Types of Questions

The majority of the questions in each section will be multiple-choice, accounting for 80% of all the questions. Each multiple-choice question will have four options to choose from, with only one correct or best answer. Remember, that there will be NO penalty for guessing wrong. So, make sure to answer each and every question.

The other type of question is the grid-in response question (20% of the total questions), which is basically a question without answer choices for you to choose from. For this type of question, you have to come up with the answer and write it in appropriately on the answer sheet. Again, NO penalty for getting wrong answers. ***One major thing to note for this is that you must write your answer in the grid-in boxes provided and also fill-in the appropriate bubbles underneath – otherwise, you won't get the credit!!***

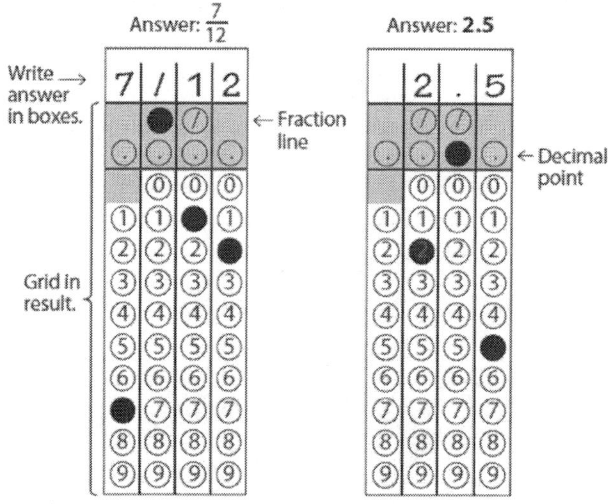

Now let's take a further look at what each of the topics actually tests.

Heart of Algebra

The point of this category is to see if you can demonstrate both procedural skill and a thorough understanding of linear equations, linear functions, and linear equalities. This is accomplished by asking you to solve straightforward questions or challenging questions. Remember that a lot of these concepts can and will be asked in many different ways. So, it's a good idea to practice with as many questions as you can, to get an idea of how to solve the same concepts in different contexts.

Here, we have outlined these concepts:

Topics and Concepts Covered
Basic Algebra • **Substituting and evaluating expressions** • **Writing algebraic expressions** • **Dependent & independent variables** • **Combining like terms** • **Interpreting linear expressions** • **Division by zero** • **One-variable linear equations** • **One-variable linear inequalities** • **Dimensional analysis for converting units** • **Two-variable linear equations** • **Ordered-pair solutions** • **X-intercepts and y-intercepts** • **Slope, Point-slope form, Standard form**

It is important to note that many Heart of Algebra questions will ask to solve for the following:

1. Define one or more variables

2. Determine the algebraic relationship between the variables
3. Solve for the required variable
4. Interpret the results to answer what the question is specifically asking

There will be a total of 19 questions for this category – 11 for the Calculator portion and 8 for the No-Calculator portion.

Problem Solving and Data Analysis

This section tests your ability to understand and represent data. This means that you have to pay attention to things such as units, measurements, ratios, trends, and principles of statistics. Some questions may be as simple as reading a value off of a graph, whereas, other questions may ask you to calculate something, like the probability of occurrence of a particular event. You will definitely have to know how to read data from line graphs, bar graphs, histograms, box-and-whisker plots, scatterplots, and two-way tables (categorical data). Here is a table of all the concepts covered in this section:

Topics and Concepts Covered
• Ratios and proportions **• Scatterplots, tables, and graphs** **- Describing trends** **- Independent vs Dependent variables** **- Analyze presented data** **- Line graphs, Bar graphs, Histograms, Box-and-Whisker Plots** **- Determine if it's a linear, quadratic, or non-linear function** **- Draw conclusions** **• Categorical data** **• Probabilities** **- Independent vs Dependent events** **- Mutually exclusive events** **• Experimental interpretation** **• Statistics** **- Medan, median, mode** **- Standard deviation, outliers** **- Precision vs accuracy** **- Margin of error** **- Confidence interval** **- Randomization of sample vs non-randomization**

For some concepts, you simply have to understand them, rather, than calculate them. For example, you will not be expected to calculate standard deviation, but, will be expected to know that a large standard deviation means the data is more spread out from the mean. ***You will NOT be asked to calculate standard deviation, margin of error, or confidence intervals. But, you must understand what these concepts mean.*** Don't worry; we have designed some awesome statistics questions that should prepare you really well for the stats topics. Another important thing to note here is that in statistics, confidence intervals other than 95% can be used, but the SAT questions will always use 95% confidence levels.)

There will be a total of 17 questions for this category – all for the Calculator portion.

Passport to Advanced Math

This category is all about understanding the structure of expressions and being able to manipulate them to solve for different variables. This also means that you have to understand what the variables represent. Basically, this section tests concepts that build on the concepts tested in the Heart of Algebra category. You are further expected to know the basics of equations, functions, and polynomial algebra. Yes, this means that all those things you hate – fractions, radicals, and exponents – are all tested!

Topics and Concepts Covered

Advanced Algebra
• **Functions**
  - **Parent functions, function notation**
  - **Domain, range, max, min, vertex, intercepts**
  - **End behavior, asymptotes**
  - **Graphing, transformation**
  - **Average rate of change**
  - **Interval where it's negative or positive**
• **Linear equations and functions word problems**
• **Systems of linear equations**
• **Two-variable linear inequalities**
• **Absolute value equations, functions, and inequalities**
• **Expressions with rational exponents and radicals**
• **Exponential growth and decay**
• **Polynomials and polynomial factorization**
• **Quadratic equations and functions**
  - **Factoring**
  - **Completing the square**
  - **Quadratic formula**
• **Rational and irrational numbers**
• **Evaluating expressions with unknown variables**
• **Manipulating expressions with unknown variables**
• **Reasoning about expressions with unknown variables**

The SAT Math test uses the following Cartesian plane assumptions for any graph on the xy-plane:

- The axes are perpendicular and the scales are linear.
- The values on the horizontal axis increase as you move to the right.
- The values on the vertical axis increase as you move up.

Note that this means that you CANNOT assume that the size of the units or measurements on the two axes is the same (unless the question specifically states that they are).

When you begin your prep for the SAT math section, make sure you master Heart of Algebra before moving on to this section.

There will be a total of 16 questions for this category – 7 for the Calculator portion and 9 for the No-Calculator portion.

Additional Topics

And finally, this section covers topics in geometry and trigonometry. It also covers complex numbers. The good thing here is that a lot of the geometry formulas are provided for you, so, you don't have to memorize a lot. ***Remember, that this section only makes up about 10% of the total Math test (6 questions out of 58).*** So, don't go spending more time prepping on this section than the other sections!

Topics and Concepts Covered
Lines and angles
- **Coordinate geometry**
- **Length formula, midpoint formula**
- **Vertical, supplementary, and complementary angles**
- **Interior angles, exterior angles**
- **Properties of parallel lines and perpendicular lines**
Triangles
- **Right triangles, equilateral triangles, isosceles triangles**
- **Pythagorean theorem**
- **Congruency and similarity**
- **Properties of triangles, triangle inequality**
Circles
- **Equation of a circle**
- **Radius, diameter, circumference, area**
- **Arc length and sector area**
- **Central angle, tangents, chords**
Other shapes
- **Squares and polygons**
Trigonometry
- **Sine, Cosine, Tan (SOHCAHTOA)**
- **Convert between angles and radians**
Complex numbers

One important thing to note in this section is that figures ARE drawn to scale unless explicitly stated otherwise (which is totally opposite from the Old SAT).

There will be a total 6 questions for this category – 3 for the Calculator portion and 3 for the No-Calculator portion.

Most Commonly Tested Topics

In this part, we wanted to delve into what this SAT Math test really focuses on. If we can find which concepts are commonly tested and which aren't, we can make our studying and prep work that much more efficient and productive.

Here's what we did:

- We went through the Math Sections of all 4 released tests from CollegeBoard and wrote down which concept was being tested for each and every question.
- We came up with a total of 26 concepts that showed up repeatedly across the 4 tests, which totalled to 232 questions.
- We tallied up all the questions according to the concept they tested.
- We calculated the frequency by dividing the number of times a concept showed up across the 4 tests by the total number of questions we looked at (232).

Caveat

But first, remember that all of this should be taken with a grain of salt for the following reasons:

- This data is only based off of 4 CollegeBoard tests – so the sample isn't really that large, which makes our results less accurate.
- Just because I say "68% of the tested concepts will be from the first 11 concepts" doesn't mean that that is exactly what you will see on the real thing. It is simply an analysis of what we found to be the case with the 4 released tests from CollegeBoard.
- All the percentages are from these 4 released CollegeBoard Tests and we are assuming that CollegeBoard will test in a similar manner on the real administered tests. So, we are trying to make predictions based off of these stats – nothing stated here is a 100% for sure thing.
- There were a few questions for which it seemed like they were testing a combination of concepts, rather than just one concept explicitly. For this type of question, we used our judgement to decide which concept it was 'most importantly' testing.

Analysis

First, here are the tables to show which topics were tested on each of the four released College Board tests and how frequently:

Practice Test 1

Heart of Algebra Concepts	# of Questions
Substituting and evaluating expressions	3
Writing algebraic expressions	3
Interpreting linear expression (equation or graph form)	4
System of linear equations	4
Slope of a line, point-slope form, standard equation of a line	1
One variable or system of linear inequalities	4

Problem Solving and Data Analysis Concepts	# of Questions
Describing trends and max/min points on graphs	3
Ratios and proportions (including direct vs inverse relationships)	8
Independent vs dependent variable (including labelling axes)	1
Statistics	1
Probability	1
Averages, average rate of change, percentages	3

Passport to Advanced Math	# of Questions
Polynomial expressions and factorization	2
Manipulating expressions with unknown variables	2
Evaluating expressions with unknown variables	3
Function notation	1
Rational and radical expressions	2
Quadratic equations and functions (including roots, restrictions, factors)	4
Exponential functions (including compound interest equations)	2

Additional Topics	# of Questions
Complex numbers	1
Triangles and angles	1
Lines and angles	1
Trigonometry	1
Equation of a circle	1
Volumes and areas	1

Practice Test 2

Heart of Algebra Concepts	# of Questions
Substituting and evaluating expressions	4
Writing algebraic expressions	4
Interpreting linear expression (equation or graph form)	2
System of linear equations	2
Slope of a line, point-slope form, standard equation of a line	4
One variable or system of linear inequalities	3

Problem Solving and Data Analysis Concepts	# of Questions
Describing trends and max/min points on graphs and tables	2
Ratios and proportions (including direct vs inverse relationships)	5
Independent vs dependent variable (including labelling axes)	
Statistics	3
Probability	1
Averages, average rate of change, percentages	4
Interpreting complex expressions	2

Passport to Advanced Math	# of Questions
Polynomial expressions and factorization	2
Manipulating expressions with unknown variables	2
Evaluating expressions with unknown variables	1
Function notation	2
Rational, exponents, and radical expressions	3
Quadratic equations and functions (including roots, restrictions, factors)	5
Exponential functions (including compound interest equations)	1

Additional Topics	# of Questions
Complex numbers	1
Triangles and angles	1
Lines and angles	
Trigonometry	
Circles (equation of a circle, circumference, area, radians, arcs, sector areas)	3
Volumes and areas	1

<u>Practice Test 3</u>

Heart of Algebra Concepts	# of Questions
Substituting and evaluating expressions	3
Writing algebraic expressions	4
Interpreting linear expression (equation or graph form)	2
System of linear equations	6
Slope of a line, point-slope form, standard equation of a line	3
One variable or system of linear inequalities	1

Problem Solving and Data Analysis Concepts	# of Questions
Describing trends and max/min points on graphs and tables	3
Ratios and proportions (including direct vs inverse relationships)	4
Independent vs dependent variable (including labelling axes)	
Statistics	2
Probability	2
Weighted averages, average rate of change, percentages	5
Interpreting complex expressions	1

Passport to Advanced Math	# of Questions
Polynomial expressions and factorization	3
Manipulating expressions with unknown variables	2
Evaluating expressions with unknown variables	1
Function notation	1
Rational, exponents, and radical expressions	2
Quadratic equations and functions (including roots, restrictions, factors, behavior)	6
Exponential functions (including growth, decay, and compound interest equations)	1

Additional Topics	# of Questions
Complex numbers	
Triangles and angles	1
Lines and angles	1
Trigonometry	2
Circles (equation of a circle, circumference, area, radians, arcs, sector areas)	1
Volumes and areas	1

<u>Practice Test 4</u>

Heart of Algebra Concepts	# of Questions
Substituting and evaluating expressions	4
Writing algebraic expressions	4
Interpreting linear expression (equation or graph form)	3
System of linear equations	3
Slope of a line, point-slope form, standard equation of a line	2
One variable or system of linear inequalities	3

Problem Solving and Data Analysis Concepts	# of Questions
Describing trends and max/min points on graphs and tables	8
Ratios and proportions (including direct vs inverse relationships)	5
Independent vs dependent variable (including labelling axes)	
Statistics	1
Probability	1
Weighted averages, average rate of change, percentages	2
Interpreting complex expressions	

Passport to Advanced Math	# of Questions
Polynomial expressions and factorization	5
Manipulating expressions with unknown variables	1
Evaluating expressions with unknown variables	2
Function notation	1
Rational, exponents, and radical expressions	
Quadratic equations and functions (including roots, restrictions, factors, behavior)	5
Exponential functions (including growth, decay, and compound interest equations)	2

Additional Topics	# of Questions
Complex numbers	3
Triangles and angles	4
Lines and angles	2
Trigonometry	4
Circles (equation of a circle, circumference, area, radians, arcs, sector areas)	7
Volumes and areas	4

So, we took all this data and found the percentage that each topic was tested in across all four practice tests. Here, are the results:

Concept	# of Questions	% of Total Questions (232)
Ratios and proportions (including direct vs inverse relationships)	22	9%
Quadratic equations and functions (including roots, restrictions, factors, behavior)	20	9%
Describing trends and max/min points on graphs and tables	16	7%
System of linear equations	15	6%
Writing algebraic expressions	15	6%
Substituting and evaluating expressions	14	6%
Weighted averages, average rate of change, percentages	14	6%
Polynomial expressions and factorization	12	5%
Interpreting linear expression (equation or graph form)	11	5%
One variable or system of linear inequalities	11	5%
Slope of a line, point-slope form, standard equation of a line	10	4%
Circles (equation of a circle, circumference, area, radians, arcs, sector areas)	7	3%
Evaluating expressions with unknown variables	7	3%
Manipulating expressions with unknown variables	7	3%
Rational, exponents, and radical expressions	7	3%
Statistics	7	3%
Exponential functions (including growth, decay, and compound interest equations)	6	3%
Function notation	5	2%
Probability	5	2%
Triangles and angles	4	2%
Trigonometry	4	2%
Volumes and areas	4	2%
Complex numbers	3	1%
Interpreting complex expressions	3	1%
Lines and angles	2	1%
Independent vs dependent variable (including labelling axes)	1	0%

The first 11 concepts:

Concept	Count	Percent
Ratios and proportions (including direct vs inverse relationships)	22	9%
Quadratic equations and functions (including roots, restrictions, factors, behavior)	20	9%
Describing trends and max/min points on graphs and tables	16	7%
System of linear equations	15	6%
Writing algebraic expressions	15	6%
Substituting and evaluating expressions	14	6%
Weighted averages, average rate of change, percentages	14	6%
Polynomial expressions and factorization	12	5%
Interpreting linear expression (equation or graph form)	11	5%
One variable or system of linear inequalities	11	5%
Slope of a line, point-slope form, standard equation of a line	10	4%

- The first 11 concepts make up 68% of the questions – which means that for any given math test of 58 questions, 40 of those questions would test these concepts.
- The last 15 concepts only make up 31% of the questions – which means that for any given math test of 58 questions, 18 of those questions would test these concepts.
- Out of the first 11 concepts, 6 of the concepts are Heart of Algebra concepts, accounting for 32% or about 1/3 of all tested concepts.
- Out of the first 11 concepts, 3 of the concepts are Problem Solving and Data Analysis concepts, accounting for 22% of all tested concepts.
- Out of the first 11 concepts, 2 of the concepts are Passport to Advanced Math concepts, accounting for 14% of all tested concepts.

The next 7 concepts:

Concept	Count	Percent
Circles (equation of a circle, circumference, area, radians, arcs, sector areas)	7	3%
Evaluating expressions with unknown variables	7	3%
Manipulating expressions with unknown variables	7	3%
Rational, exponents, and radical expressions	7	3%
Statistics	7	3%
Exponential functions (including growth, decay, and compound interest equations)	6	3%
Function notation	5	2%

I didn't want to include Function Notation; however, I felt that this concept is sooooo easy, compared to the last 8 concepts, that I might as well include it with this group. So, this next chunk of concepts comprises 20% of tested concepts.

- Questions about circles, part of the Additional Topics category, appear to be the most tested of the Additional Topics concepts.
- 5 of these concepts are from Passport to Advanced Math, accounting for 14% of all tested concepts.
- Statistics only makes up 3% of all tested concepts.

The last 8 concepts:

Probability	5	2%
Triangles and angles	4	2%
Trigonometry	4	2%
Volumes and areas	4	2%
Complex numbers	3	1%
Interpreting complex expressions	3	1%
Lines and angles	2	1%
Independent vs dependent variable (including labelling axes)	1	0%

- 5 of the concepts are from the Additional Topics category.
- 3 of the concepts are from Problem Solving and Data Analysis.

Results

- Just 6 Heart of Algebra concepts account for 32% of all tested concepts.
- Combined from above, just 4 Problem Solving and Data Analysis concepts make up 25% of all tested concepts.
- Combined from above, just 7 Passport to Advanced Math concepts make up 28% of all tested concepts.
- 18 concepts make up 88% of all tested concepts. This is equal to about 51 questions out of 58. This gives a raw score of about 690 according to the raw score conversion tables made available by CollegeBoard.
- 17 of these concepts make up 85% of all tested concepts. This is equal to about 49 questions out of 58. This gives a raw score of about 710 according to the raw score conversion tables made available by CollegeBoard.
- The 11 most common concepts make up 68% of all tested concepts. This is equal to about 40 questions out of 58. This gives a raw score of about 610 according to the raw score conversion tables made available by CollegeBoard.

Discussion

So, what does all of this mean? How can it help you? Well, it really depends on what your specific situation and goals are. If you are in a time crunch, for example, then it might be wise to study the 11 most commonly tested concepts, so, that you can still get a score around 600. And if you have a bit more time, then study the first 18 concepts so that you have a chance at a 700. However, if you do have a lot of time on your hands, then it would be wise to begin with the concepts outlined in this analysis of the 4 released CollegeBoard tests. This would allow you to start doing really well on your practice tests, early in your prep, giving you a huge confidence and motivation boost. Then, you can focus on the rarer concepts, common mistakes, and harder material to go from 700 to 800.

Another thing to point out is that out of all of the Additional Topics concepts, it seems that concepts related to circles are the most important. So, if you really hate geometry and don't want to bother with triangles and such, at the very least, you should study up circles.

In Heart of Algebra, we were quite surprised to see some topics so heavily tested. For example, systems of linear equations; each of the 4 tests from CollegeBoard had anywhere between 2 to 6 questions on just this concept. Most of the time they gave you both equations, but rarely they asked you to come up with the equations also.

Writing linear algebraic equations from word problems is also a big one. The next few heavily tested concepts were ratios & proportions, polynomials, quadratics, and being able to read graphs and tables for things such as trends, max/min points, and specific values. So, without a doubt, do not go into the test without being comfortable with these things.

In terms of difficulty of questions, it seemed that, generally, the difficulty increased as you got further along in the math section. Section 4 (the calculator portion) had more difficult questions than Section 3. However, a lot of the questions in Section 4 could easily be solved without using a calculator. So, depending on how much you rely on your calculator, you may or may not use it much for section 4.

Overall, I believe that the SAT Math test is fair and maybe even easier than the old SAT math. There are no tricks and strangely worded questions. You've learned the majority of these concepts in school - mainly Grade 11 Functions. And the questions are exactly as you've seen them in school also. I think this familiarity of these questions will help decrease anxiety for many students. If you have done well in math at school, then you will definitely do well on this SAT Math test. If you haven't, then you'll have to work a little harder to review all the concepts that you're weak in and show colleges that you have improved in math by doing well on the SAT Math test.

I hope that these tables and analysis have given you a little more insight into the SAT Math test, making it a little more predictable and less scary. If you find that you are lacking in certain skills, then there are great resources to help with your review. Our main goal is to use these findings to create the best practice tests we can for students. As CollegeBoard releases more tests and we can glean more information from student experiences, our tests will get better and better going into the future.

Strategy

General Strategies on the Test

1. **Process of Elimination:** This strategy is golden when you're a bit stuck. If you weren't able to solve the question and find the right answer right away, then start by eliminating the most wrong choices right away – and there are usually one or two of them for every question. Since, you only have four choices to begin with; this really helps narrow it down. After eliminating two choices, even if you have to totally guess, you're chances to guess correctly are 50%.
2. **Plug-in Answer Choices:** This is another thing to try when you're stuck. Pick one of the answer choices (usually the middle one is the best one to go with) and plug it in to the question. You can usually get the answer this way within two guesses, because the first guess will give you a good idea of what answer choice to try next.
3. **Substitute Numbers for Variables:** Sometimes, when you're given a formula and asked to manipulate it, you substitute easy numbers into it to make sure you did it right.
4. **Target Easy Questions First:** This strategy works for those that are very nervous and need a confidence boost early on. You can quickly flip through the section and find which questions you think are easy and do them first. What constitutes an easy question? Well, it's whatever topic you think you're most comfortable with and whether you can get the answer under 30 seconds. That seems like a very short amount of time, but it's not. 30 seconds is a long time. Try counting to 30 seconds right now and you'll see. If you can't get the answer in 30 seconds, then it's not an easy question. Try to notice this during your practice and while you are doing the practice tests in this book. You will notice that you get the easy questions almost immediately. After you're certain you've got all the easy questions, move on to the harder ones.
5. **Save Data Tables For The End:** These questions usually want you to analyze the data and that can take you 30 seconds to a minute at least. Then they want you to do something with that data, which will take you another 30 seconds to a minute at least. So, although not hard, these questions are time consuming. Save them for the end. Time management is key to doing well on this test. Do the same for any complicated graph question. Sometimes, though, the question will be very simple – they may just want you to read a value off the graph, which you can do very quickly.
6. **Remember that you can mark-up and write all over your test booklet** – so make sure to actually cross things out that you want to eliminate, put a star besides ones that you think are hard, write down things that you've memorized, and whatever else you feel will help you.
7. **Read each and every question carefully** and try to come up with the answer before looking at the answers. Then look at every answer before picking the right one.
8. **Memorize common formulas and facts.** This will naturally help you do questions quicker. This includes memorizing all the formulas provided to you on the reference sheet. This prevents wasting time by flipping back and forth between your question and the reference sheet.
9. **Try not to depend on your calculator too much.** Most questions on the SAT math test can be done without using a calculator. We recommend using the calculator for mainly questions with really ugly numbers that make it hard to do mental math.

How to Get a 500+ Score

Getting a score of 500 should be very easy on this test. You just have to know all the basic concepts.

Number of Correct Questions: 22 - 26

Percentage: 38% - 45%

Study Plan

- 1 hour a day to review concepts for 2 months
- 30 minutes a day to do practice questions
- At least 4 timed math practice tests

Main focus of studying:

- Heart of Algebra
- Top 11 concepts from our analysis

How to Get a 600+ Score

Getting a score of 600 will require a little more effort but will also be relatively easy to accomplish.

Number of Correct Questions: 32 – 38

Percentage: 55% - 66%

Study Plan

- 1 - 2 hours a day to review concepts for 2 months
- 30 minutes a day to do practice questions
- At least 6 timed math practice tests

Main focus of studying:

- Heart of Algebra
- Passport to Advanced Math
- Top 18 concepts from our analysis

How to Get a 700+ Score

Getting a score of 700 will be harder to accomplish and will require a good amount of effort. We really recommend you start prep early and leave about 4 months to get to this score and above (unless you're very good at math already). From our analysis, we recommend that you study and be comfortable with all 26 of the most commonly tested concepts. You should also thoroughly review Basic Algebra and Advanced Algebra, which covers things such as quadratics, polynomials, rational expressions, radicals, exponents, graphs, functions, and more. This will prepare you very well for the math test and you should be able to get almost all the questions. You can get the hardest questions wrong. Even if you miss a handful of questions, you can still end up with a 700+ score.

Number of Correct Questions: 43 – 50

Percentage: 74% - 86%

Study Plan

- 2 - 3 hours a day to review concepts for 2 - 4 months
- 30 minutes - 1 hour a day to do practice questions
- At least 8 timed math practice tests

Main focus of studying:

- Heart of Algebra
- Passport to Advanced Math
- Problem Solving and Data Analysis
- All 26 commonly tested concepts from our analysis

How to Get a Perfect 800 Score

Getting a perfect 800 score will be a challenge and will require a tremendous effort. BUT, it's totally doable. You don't have to be a genius to get a perfect 800; you just have to be a hard and disciplined worker. We really recommend you start prep early and leave about 4 months to get to this score. From our analysis, we recommend that you study and be comfortable with all 26 of the most commonly tested concepts, everything outlined for the 'How To Get A 700+ Score' section and also all the Additional Topics concepts tested on the SAT. That means that you should definitely be comfortable with trigonometry, geometry, and complex numbers. Three out of four of the practice tests, released by CollegeBoard, show that you need to get all 58 questions correct in order to get 800 – even missing one can drop you down to a 790. The key to this is going to be time management, targeting your weaknesses with practice tests, eliminating careless mistakes, and doing as many timed SAT math practice tests as possible.

Number of Correct Questions: 57 – 58

Percentage: 98% - 100%

Study Plan

- 2 - 3 hours a day to review concepts for 2 - 4 months
- 30 minutes - 1 hour a day to do practice questions
- At least 10 timed math practice tests

Main focus of studying:

- Heart of Algebra
- Passport to Advanced Math
- Problem Solving and Data Analysis
- Additional Topics

- All 26 commonly tested concepts from our analysis

How to Use Practice Tests

- **Real Conditions:** Always do the practice test under real conditions. Go to a quiet room, time yourself, and complete the whole test without any breaks. Also, it's a good idea to do the practice test at the same time as when you will give your SAT – usually that's around 8 am. This will make sure that you get used to having to think this early on in the day.
- **Targeted Practice:** Practice tests (and any practice questions you do) can let you know what your major and minor weaknesses are. Always analyze your results to find the reason why you got any question wrong (this includes questions you had to guess on). Categorize your weaknesses based on concept or question type. Then review those concepts, starting from the ones you get wrong the most and working your way down. And, of course, make sure to go back and re-do the questions you couldn't do to make sure that you can do them.
- **Concept Review vs Time Management:** Practice tests can let you know whether or not your weakness is time management. The way you do this is to start noticing if you are always rushing near the end of a section. If you feel like you're rushing the last 5 or so questions, then you have a time management issue. You can also check this by doing a practice test where you time yourself, but don't stop a section once the time has run out. Keep going and finish the section, but make a note of all the questions that you had to do once the allotted time passed. Then when you score your test, break it up into two scores: one for the questions you finished within the allotted time and one score that includes the questions that you needed extra time for. Then compare the two scores. If you see that there is a difference of 50 or more points, then you definitely have a time management issue. And if there is almost no difference, then your timing is excellent and you should focus more on the concepts.
- **Careless Mistakes:** Everyone makes careless mistakes. Practice tests give us a great glimpse at what these mistakes are. Go through each practice test and find the careless mistakes you made. Then write down on a piece of paper what that careless mistake was and make sure to read that piece of paper every day. The whole premise behind careless mistakes is that you simply don't notice them when you make them. So, being more aware of them should help eliminate them.
- **When to take them:** Take one practice test at the beginning of your prep to see where you stand and what you already know really well. This could tell you where to start your prep. For example, if you got most of the algebra questions right, but a lot of the quadratic questions wrong, then you would start your prep by reviewing quadratics concepts. After this first practice test, you should not take any more practice tests for 2 – 4 weeks, while you are reviewing concepts. Give yourself some time to learn a chunk of concepts and practice them on questions. Then, start doing 1 practice test every weekend. Remember to analyze the results of each practice test you do and target those weaknesses for the following week, before you do the next practice test. That way you will definitely see improvements every week and it will give you a big confidence and motivation boost.

How To Score The Tests

1. Add up the number of correct answers you got for Section 3 (no calculator) and Section 4 (calculator). Remember, there is no penalty for wrong answers. This is your raw score.
2. Use the raw score conversion table below to convert your raw score into a scaled score from 200 – 800.

Raw Score Conversion Table:

Raw Score	Scaled Score	Raw Score	Scaled Score	Raw Score	Scaled Score
0	200	21	460	42	630
1	200	22	470	43	640
2	210	23	480	44	650
3	230	24	480	45	660
4	240	25	490	46	670
5	260	26	500	47	670
6	280	27	510	48	680
7	290	28	520	49	690
8	310	29	520	50	700
9	320	30	530	51	710
10	330	31	540	52	730
11	340	32	550	53	740
12	360	33	560	54	750
13	370	34	560	55	760
14	380	35	570	56	780
15	390	36	580	57	790
16	410	37	590	58	800
17	420	38	600		
18	430	39	600		
19	440	40	610		
20	450	41	620		

6 Full Length Math Practice Tests + Answer Keys + Full Solutions

IMPORTANT

All math tests are in the format of Section 3 and Section 4.

Section 3 does **not** permit a calculator.

Section 4 allows a calculator.

There is a reference sheet at the beginning of each section.

TEST 1

ANSWER SHEET

Section 3

1 A B C D	4 A B C D	7 A B C D	10 A B C D	13 A B C D
2 A B C D	5 A B C D	8 A B C D	11 A B C D	14 A B C D
3 A B C D	6 A B C D	9 A B C D	12 A B C D	15 A B C D

16	17	18	19	20
/	/	/	/	/
.	.	.	.	.
0	0	0	0	0
1	1	1	1	1
2	2	2	2	2
3	3	3	3	3
4	4	4	4	4
5	5	5	5	5
6	6	6	6	6
7	7	7	7	7
8	8	8	8	8
9	9	9	9	9

Section 4

21 A B C D	27 A B C D	33 A B C D	39 A B C D	45 A B C D
22 A B C D	28 A B C D	34 A B C D	40 A B C D	46 A B C D
23 A B C D	29 A B C D	35 A B C D	41 A B C D	47 A B C D
24 A B C D	30 A B C D	36 A B C D	42 A B C D	48 A B C D
25 A B C D	31 A B C D	37 A B C D	43 A B C D	49 A B C D
26 A B C D	32 A B C D	38 A B C D	44 A B C D	50 A B C D

51

/
.
0
1
2
3
4
5
6
7
8
9

52

/
.
0
1
2
3
4
5
6
7
8
9

53

/
.
0
1
2
3
4
5
6
7
8
9

54

/
.
0
1
2
3
4
5
6
7
8
9

55

/
.
0
1
2
3
4
5
6
7
8
9

56

/
.
0
1
2
3
4
5
6
7
8
9

57

/
.
0
1
2
3
4
5
6
7
8
9

58

/
.
0
1
2
3
4
5
6
7
8
9

Section 3

Math Test – No Calculator
Allotted Time: 25 Minutes
Number of Questions: 20

Calculator **NOT** permitted.

Reference Formulas

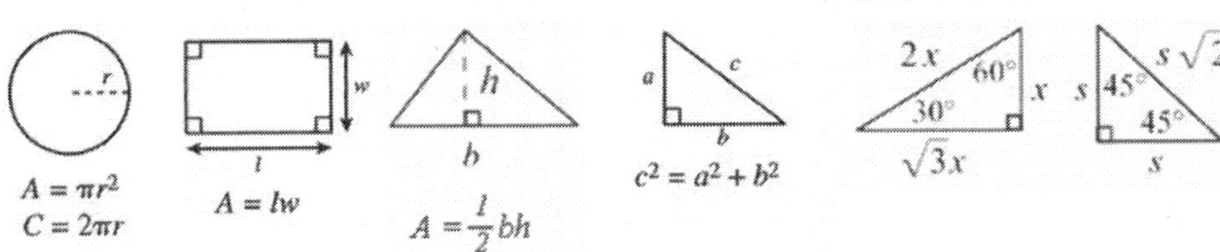

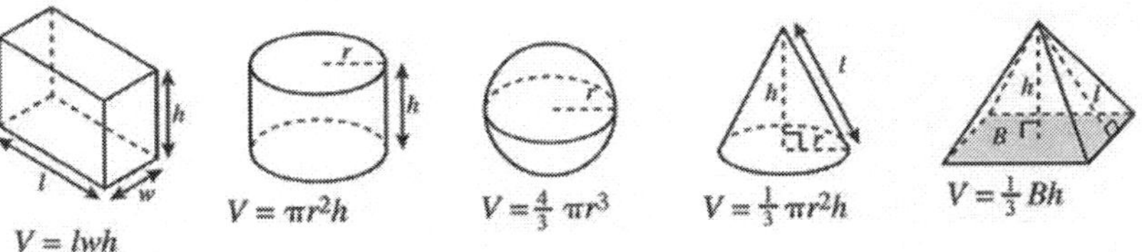

The number of degrees of arc in a circle is 360.
The number of radians of arc in a circle is 2π.
The sum of the measures in degrees of the angles of a triangle is 180.

1. If $\frac{4x-k}{3} = -k$ and $k = -3$, what is the value of $4x + 3$?

   A) 7
   B) 8
   C) 9
   D) 10

2. For $i = \sqrt{-1}$, what is the quotient $\frac{6-2i}{2+5i}$?

   A) $3 - \frac{2}{5}i$
   B) $4 - 3i$
   C) $\frac{1}{5} + \frac{2}{3}i$
   D) $\frac{2}{29} - \frac{34}{29}i$

3. The hotel Sea View has m floors with n rooms on each floor, and 4 beds in each room. The hotel Sunny Beach has s floors with t rooms on each floor, and 3 beds in each room. What is the total number of beds in both hotels?

   A) $4mn + 3st$
   B) $m + 4n + s + 3t$
   C) $7(mn + st)$
   D) $12(mn + st)$

4. The elevator is moving down at the constant speed. The altitude of the elevator above the ground is represented by the equation $H = 12 - 0.25t$. What is the meaning of value 0.25 in this equation?

   A) The initial altitude of the elevator
   B) The movement of the elevator in the unit of time t
   C) The altitude of the elevator after 12 seconds
   D) The time needed elevator to lower on the ground floor

5. $(7xy^2 - 3xy + 6x) + (-5xy^2 + 2x + 3xy)$

   Which of the following is equivalent to the expression above?

   A) $2xy(y - 4)$
   B) $2xy(y + 4)$
   C) $2x(y - 2)(y + 2)$
   D) $2x(y^2 + 4)$

6.

$$C = 8 + 4m$$

Liam uses the model above to estimate the cost C of the taxi drive after m miles passed. Based on the model, what is the increase in price after one mile passed?

   A) \$2
   B) \$4
   C) \$6
   D) \$8

7.

$$v = \sqrt{\frac{GM}{r}}$$

The formula above gives the orbital velocity *v* of the object which mass is *M* and distance from the center of Earth is *r*. Which of the following gives *r* in terms of *G*, *M* and *v* ? (Note: G is gravitational constant 6.67×10^{-11})

   A) $\frac{G}{Mv^2}$
   B) $\frac{Gv^2}{M}$
   C) $\frac{GM}{v^2}$
   D) $\frac{M}{Gv^2}$

8. If $\frac{a}{3b} = -6$, what is the value of $\frac{a}{2} + 9b$?

A) 0
B) 1
C) 2
D) 3

9.

$$\frac{x}{2} - (y+1) = x$$
$$x - \frac{y}{3} = 5$$

What is the solution (x, y) to the system of linear equations above?

A) (4,3)
B) (-4,3)
C) (4,-3)
D) (-4,-3)

10.

$$f(x) = \sqrt{x^2 - 2a}$$

For the function *f* defined above, *a* is a constant and *f*(5) = 3. What is the value of *f*(−5) ?

A) 1
B) 2
C) 3
D) 4

11.

$$m = 7 + 0.5h$$
$$n = 9 + 0.25h$$

In the equations above, *m* and *n* represent the temperature, in degrees Celsius, in New York and Boston, respectively, *h* hours after sunrise. What was the temperature in New York when it was equal to the temperature in Boston?

A) 10
B) 11
C) 12
D) 13

12. Which of the following points lies on a line in the xy-plane which passes through the points (-4,-2) and (1,-8)?

A) (-9,4)
B) (9,-4)
C) (-4,9)
D) (4,-9)

13. Which of the following is equivalent to $\frac{1}{\frac{1}{x-1} - \frac{1}{x+1}}$?

A) $\frac{x^2+1}{2}$

B) $\frac{x^2-1}{2}$

C) $\frac{1-x^2}{2}$

D) $\frac{x^2}{2}$

14. If $2x + 3y - z = 10$, what is the value of $\frac{4^x 8^y}{2^z}$?

A) 2^5
B) 4^5
C) 8^5
D) 16^5

15. If $(ax-2)(bx-5)=cx^2-19x+d$ for all values of x, and $a+b=5$, what is the value of $\sqrt{\frac{cd}{15}}$?

A) 1
B) 2
C) 3
D) 4

Student-Produced Responses

16. If $x<0$ and $x^4-81=0$, what is the value of x?

17. The height of the stick is 3 feet. Its shadow is 1 feet and 6 inches long. What is the height of the tree which shadow is 12 feet long?

18.

$$\frac{x-2}{3}+\frac{y}{2}=1+\frac{x}{4}$$
$$2x-5y=-11$$

What is the value of x in the system of equations above?

19. In a right triangle, one angle measures x^o, where $\tan x^o=\frac{15}{8}$. What is $\sin x^o$?

20. Calculate $\frac{\sqrt{4-2\sqrt{3}}+\sqrt{4+2\sqrt{3}}}{\sqrt{3}}$

Section 4

Math Test – Calculator
Allotted Time: 55 Minutes
Number of Questions: 38

Calculator **IS** allowed.

Reference Formulas

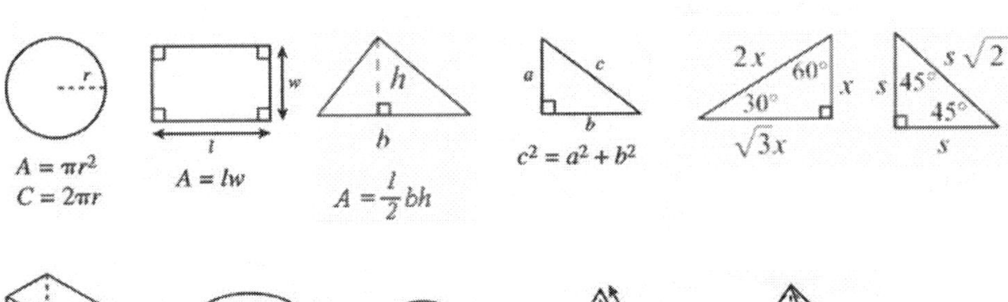

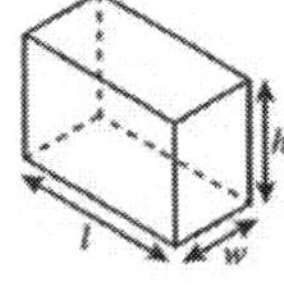

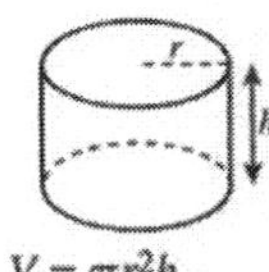

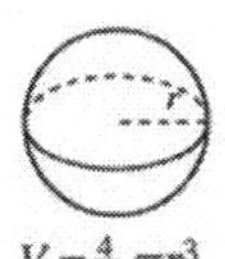

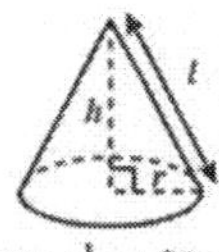

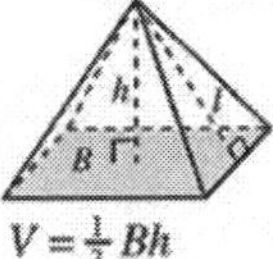

The number of degrees of arc in a circle is 360.
The number of radians of arc in a circle is 2π.
The sum of the measures in degrees of the angles of a triangle is 180.

21. The bus is traveling at different speeds. The graph below shows its speed at different times during journey. What is the average speed of the bus between the 8th and 12th minutes?

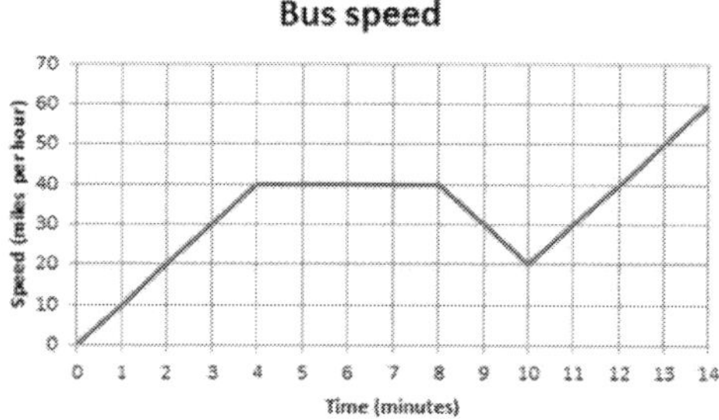

A) 22
B) 28
C) 32
D) 38

22. What is the x-intercept of a line $y = kx - \frac{5}{2}$ which is parallel to the line $x - 2y = -4$?

A) 2
B) 3
C) 4
D) 5

23.

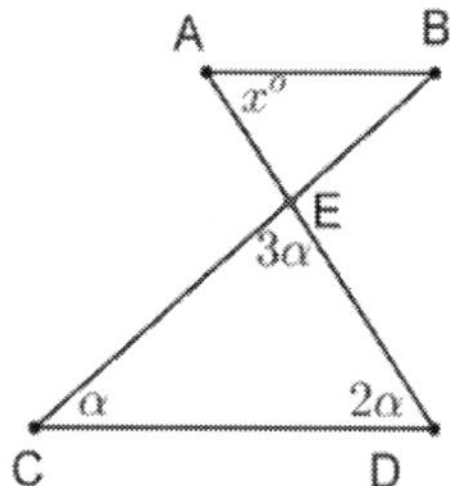

In the figure above, segments AB and CD are parallel. What is the measure of x^o?

A) 45°
B) 50°
C) 55°
D) 60°

24. If $x^2 - 6x + 9$ is 4 less than 5, and $x < 4$, what is the value of $x^2 + 3$?

A) 7
B) 8
C) 9
D) 10

25. Which of the following graphs shows no association between x and y?

A)

B)

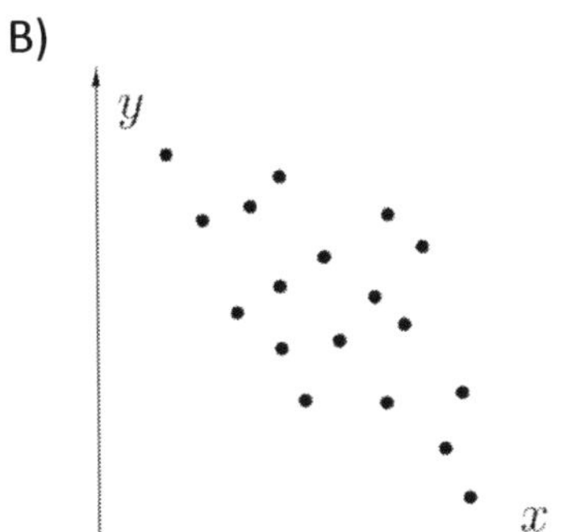

C)

D)

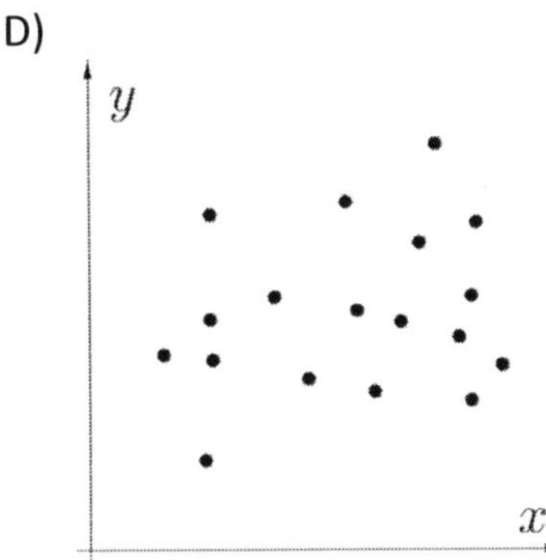

26.

$$1\ km = 1{,}000\ m$$
$$1\ hour = 60\ minutes$$
$$1\ minute = 60\ seconds$$

Men's 100 m world record is 9.58 seconds, held by Usein Bolt. What was Bolt's average speed in that race in kilometers per hour?

A) $35.58\frac{km}{h}$
B) $36.42\frac{km}{h}$
C) $37.58\frac{km}{h}$
D) $38.42\frac{km}{h}$

27.

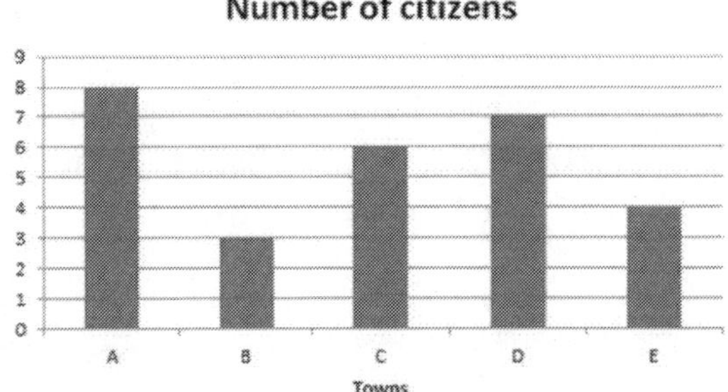

The number of citizens in 5 towns is shown in the graph above. If the average number of citizens in 5 towns is 56,000, what is an appropriate label for the vertical axis of the graph?

A) Number of citizens (in hundreds)
B) Number of citizens (in thousands)
C) Number of citizens (in ten thousands)
D) Number of citizens (in hundred thousands)

28. If $|3 - x| < 2$, what are the possible values for x?

A) $1 < x < 5$
B) $-1 < x < 5$
C) $x < 1$
D) $x < 5$

Questions 29 and 30 refer to the following information.

$$u = \frac{v + u'}{1 + \frac{vu'}{c^2}}$$

If A sees B moving at velocity v, then a velocity measured by B (u') would be seen by A as in the formula above.

29. Which of the following expresses a velocity measured by B (*u'*) in terms of the velocity that would be seen by A (*u*), and the velocity of B as seen by A (*v*)?

A) $\frac{u-v}{1+\frac{uv}{c^2}}$
B) $\frac{u-v}{1-\frac{uv}{c^2}}$
C) $\frac{u+v}{1-\frac{uv}{c^2}}$
D) $\frac{u+v}{1+\frac{uv}{c^2}}$

30. If B moves at the speed of 100,000 miles per second, what must be the speed measured by B so that it is seen by A as 110,000 miles per second?
(Note: $c \approx 300{,}000\ \frac{km}{s}$)

A) 8,363.64
B) 9,363.64
C) 10,363.64
D) 11,363.64

31. Which of the following numbers is a solution of the inequality $\frac{x-2}{3} - x \geq 1 - \frac{x+1}{6}$?

A) -3
B) -2
C) -1
D) 0

32.

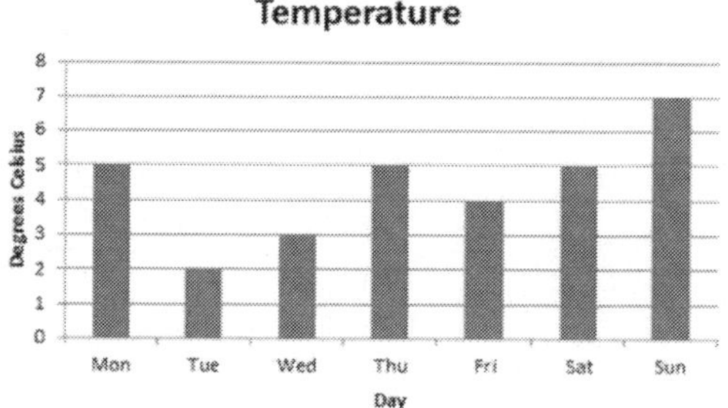

On which day was the temperature closest to the average weekly temperature?

A) Monday
B) Wednesday
C) Friday
D) Sunday

33.

		Pets			
		Dogs	Cats	Parrots	Total
Gender	Female	12	18	12	42
	Male	24	6	8	38
	Total	36	24	20	80

The table above shows the number of pets according to their gender. What is the percent of female dogs and parrots among all female pets?

A) 27%
B) 37%
C) 47%
D) 57%

34.

The number of shirts sold in April						
21	45	12	16	32	25	12
14	13	25	21	8	14	3
12	12	21	16	7	16	12
15	11	5	16	12	27	5

A T-shirt company keeps a track of how many shirts they sell daily, every month. The table above represents the number of shirts sold every day during the month of April.How much will mean change if you omit the last row?

A) 1
B) 2
C) 3
D) 4

Questions 35 and 36 refer to the following information.

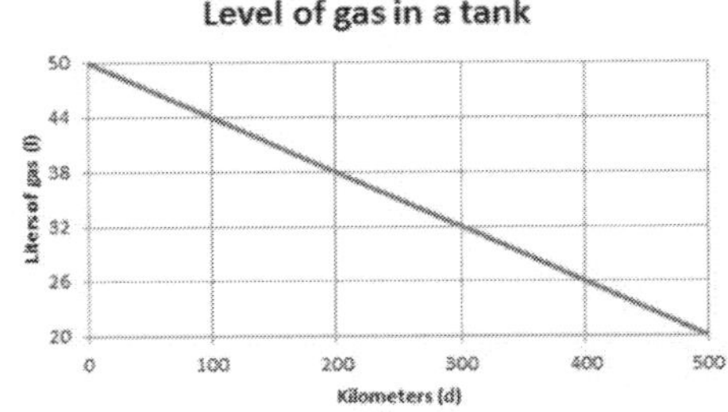

The graph above displays the level of gas in the tank *l*, in liters, depending on the distance passed *d*, in kilometers.

35. What is the level of gas in the tank after 650 kilometers?

A) 11
B) 19
C) 31
D) 39

36. How many kilometers can be passed with 1 liter of gas?

A) 16.33
B) 16.67
C) 17.33
D) 17.67

37.

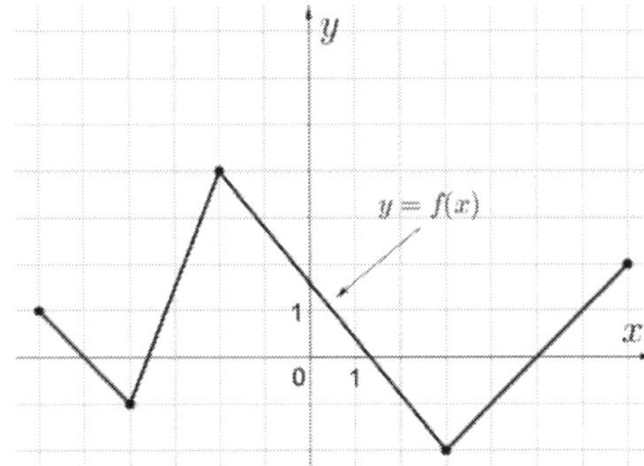

The complete graph of the function *f* is shown in the *xy*-plane above. What is the interval in which function increases?

A) $-4 < x < -2 \wedge 3 < x < 7$
B) $-4 < x < -2$
C) $3 < x < 7$
D) $-4 < x < 7$

38.

$$ax + by < a$$

What must be the value of a so that point (0,0) is NOT the solution of the inequality above?

A) $a < 0$
B) $a \leq 0$
C) $a > 0$
D) $a \geq 0$

39. Mother is 18 years older than her son. Three years ago, she was 3 times older than her son. What is the sum of their ages?

A) 42
B) 43
C) 44
D) 45

40. The price of an item increased 12%, and then decreased 12%. How many percent did the initial price change?

A) 0%
B) 1%
C) 1.44%
D) 2.56%

41.

Years of experience of employees

	Less than 10	Between 10 and 20	Between 20 and 30	More than 30	Total
Males	12	14	8	6	40
Females	6	24	16	4	50
Total	18	38	24	10	90

The table above shows the number of employees based on their years of experience. If a person is chosen at random from employees with less than 30 years of experience, what is the probability that it is a male with more than 10 years of experience?

A) $\frac{11}{20}$

B) $\frac{11}{30}$

C) $\frac{11}{40}$

D) $\frac{11}{50}$

Questions 42 and 43 refer to the following information.

Number of students at Faculty of Natural Sciences and Mathematics

Department	Year			
	2010	2011	2012	2013
Math	120	90	110	86
Physics	86	90	96	108
Biology	94	76	88	92
Chemistry	108	120	115	103

The table above lists the number of students at Faculty of Natural Sciences and Mathematics from 2010 to 2013.

42. What is the rate of change of the number of students at the Physics Department from 2011 to 2013?

A) 7
B) 8
C) 9
D) 10

43. Which department has the average number of students closest to the average number of all students from 2010 to 2013?

A) Math
B) Physics
C) Biology
D) Chemistry

44. What is the radius of a circle $x^2 + y^2 - 4x + 8y - 5 = 0$?

A) 4
B) 5
C) 6
D) 7

45.

$$P = \frac{1}{4}t^2 + t - 5$$

The profit *P* of the company, in millions of dollars, is given by the equation above, where *t* is time in years. After which year has the company started making profit?

A) 1st
B) 2nd
C) 3rd
D) 4th

46. Noah is 25% taller than Sarah. If Noah grows up for 5% of his current height, he would be tall as Joshua. How tall is Joushua, if Sarah is 160 cm tall?

A) 180 cm
B) 190 cm
C) 200 cm
D) 210 cm

47. At the entrance of the stadium, 300 visitors were pleased to put on a green hat. Later, during the rock concert, researcher took a photo of a random group of people. He counted 120 people on a photo, and 2 of them had green hats. What is the expected number of people on the stadium?

A) 10,000
B) 18,000
C) 25,000
D) 40,000

48.

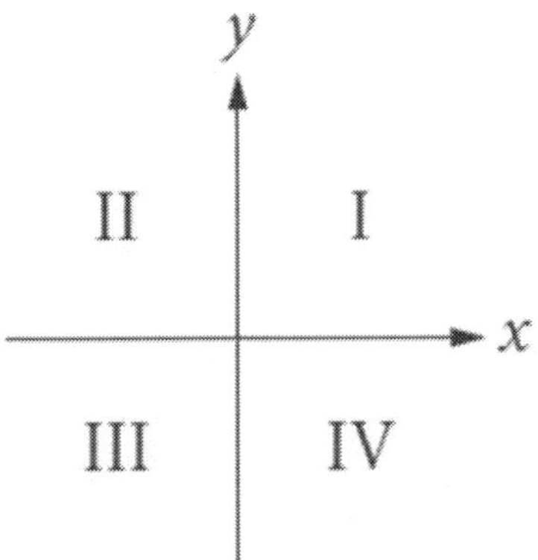

If the system of inequalities $11 - 3y < 4x$ and $4x - y > 7$ is graphed in the xy-plane above, which quadrants contain solutions to the system of inequalities?

A) I and II
B) II and III
C) III and IV
D) II, II and IV

49. If $p(x) + p(-x) = 0$, what is the value of $p(0)$?

A) 0
B) 1
C) 2
D) 3

50. What are the coordinates of the vertex of parabola which x-intercepts are -1 and 4, and y-intercept is -1?

A) $\left(\frac{1}{2}, -\frac{3}{2}\right)$
B) $\left(\frac{3}{2}, -\frac{25}{16}\right)$
C) $\left(\frac{3}{2}, -\frac{5}{4}\right)$
D) $\left(\frac{1}{2}, -\frac{5}{4}\right)$

Student-Produced Responses

51. If $\left|\frac{2-5x}{3}\right| < 4$ and $x \in N$, what is one possible value for x?

52. Sophia has $500. She wants to buy a mobile phone, which costs $240, two bags which cost $42 each, and some T-shirts which cost $12 each. At most how many T-shirts can she buy?

53.

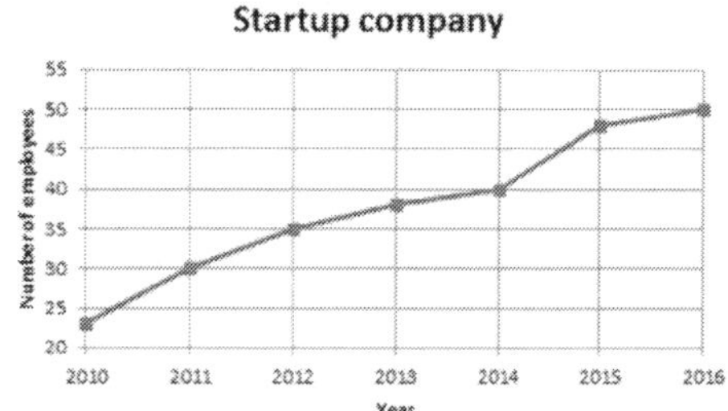

What was the rate of change of the number of employees from 2011 to 2016?

54. The distance between towns A and B is 60 miles. Joshua and Noah started biking at the same time. Joshua is biking from A to B, and Noah is biking from B to A. If Joshua bikes at the constant speed of 7 miles per hour, and Noah bikes at the constant speed of 5 miles per hour, after how many hours will they meet?

55. Ethan wants to paint a cube box in red. He can paint 32 square feet with one can of color. The price of one can of color is \$4.50. How much will it cost to paint the cube, if the volume of a cube is 1,728 cubic feet? (Round your answer to the nearest dollar).

56. For what value of x is the function $y = \frac{1}{x^4-1}$ undefined?

Questions 57 and 58 refer to the following information.

The number of employees in the company falls 6% each year. In 2010, there were 2,200 employees. The expression $2{,}200 \times (x)^t$ is used to estimate the number of employees after t years.

57. What would be the value of x in the expression if the number of employees grows 6% each year?

58. After how many years will the number of employees be less than half? (Round your answer to the whole number).

No Test Material On This Page

Test 1 Answer Key

1	C	21	C	41	C
2	D	22	D	42	C
3	A	23	D	43	A
4	B	24	A	44	B
5	D	25	D	45	C
6	B	26	C	46	D
7	C	27	C	47	B
8	A	28	A	48	A
9	C	29	B	49	A
10	C	30	D	50	B
11	B	31	A	51	1 OR 2
12	A	32	C	52	14
13	B	33	D	53	4
14	B	34	A	54	5
15	B	35	A	55	122
16	-3	36	B	56	+1 or -1
17	24	37	A	57	1.06
18	2	38	B	58	12
19	0.88 or 15/17	39	A		
20	2	40	C		

TEST 2

ANSWER SHEET

Section 3

1 A B C D
2 A B C D
3 A B C D
4 A B C D
5 A B C D
6 A B C D
7 A B C D
8 A B C D
9 A B C D
10 A B C D
11 A B C D
12 A B C D
13 A B C D
14 A B C D
15 A B C D

16

17

18

19

20

/ . 0 1 2 3 4 5 6 7 8 9

Section 4

21 A B C D
22 A B C D
23 A B C D
24 A B C D
25 A B C D
26 A B C D
27 A B C D
28 A B C D
29 A B C D
30 A B C D
31 A B C D
32 A B C D
33 A B C D
34 A B C D
35 A B C D
36 A B C D
37 A B C D
38 A B C D
39 A B C D
40 A B C D
41 A B C D
42 A B C D
43 A B C D
44 A B C D
45 A B C D
46 A B C D
47 A B C D
48 A B C D
49 A B C D
50 A B C D

51

52

53

54

55

56

57

58

Section 3

Math Test – No Calculator
Allotted Time: 25 Minutes
Number of Questions: 20

Calculator **NOT** permitted.

Reference Formulas

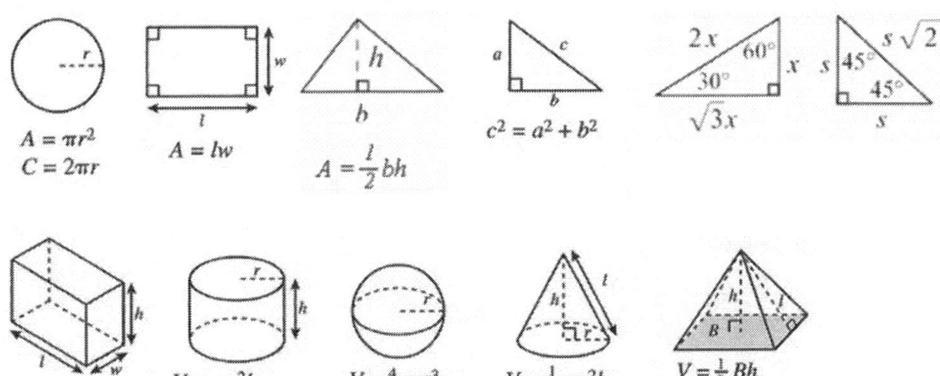

The number of degrees of arc in a circle is 360.
The number of radians of arc in a circle is 2π.
The sum of the measures in degrees of the angles of a triangle is 180.

1. In a restaurant, 4 cans of soft drinks and 5 slices of pizza cost \$12.00. In the same restaurant, 6 cans of soft drinks and 8 slices of pizza cost \$21.25. How much do you have to pay for 8 cans of soft drinks and 12 slices of pizza?

   A. \$30
   B. \$37
   C. \$35
   D. \$40

2. John and Dave were solving a problem that would reduce it to a quadratic equation. John committed an error in the constant term and found the roots to be 9 and 7 while Dave made an error in the first degree term and gave the roots as 7 and 4. If you were to check their solutions, the right equation is:

   A. $x^2 - 16x + 28 = 0$
   B. $x^2 - 12x + 32 = 0$
   C. $x^2 - 12x + 35 = 0$
   D. None of the above

3. Solve the following equation for x: $4e^{2x}$-$2e^{x}$ = 0

   A. $\log_e 2$
   B. $-\log_e 2$
   C. $\frac{1}{2}$
   D. $-\frac{1}{2}$

4. Find the integers x and y such that $\frac{1}{\sqrt{10}-3} = x + y\sqrt{10}$

   A. x = 2, y = 1
   B. x = 3, y = 2
   C. x = 3, y = 1
   D. x = 1, y = 1

5. A water tank is to be designed in the shape of a cylinder with radius "r" in meters and height "h" in meters. If the volume of the tank is 20 cubic meters, what is the total surface area of the tank in terms of radius "r"?

   A. $2\pi r^2 + 20r$
   B. $2\pi r^2 + 40r$
   C. $2\pi r^2 + 40/r$
   D. $2\pi r^2 + 20/r$

6. $(\sqrt{8} - 8)^2$ is equivalent to _____.

   A. $-16\sqrt{8} + 58$
   B. $4(9 - 2\sqrt{8})$
   C. $8(9 - 2\sqrt{8})$
   D. $9 - 2\sqrt{8}$

7. Find the value of α

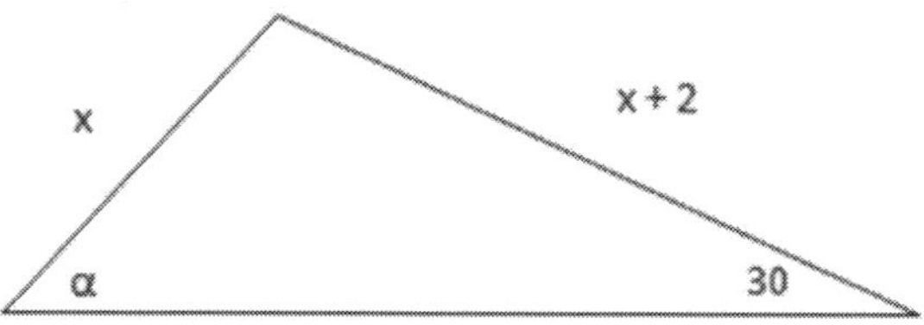

   A. $sin^{-1}\left(\frac{(x+2)}{2x}\right)$
   B. $sin^{-1}\left(\frac{(x+2)}{x}\right)$
   C. $sin^{-1}\left(\frac{(x+2)}{4x}\right)$
   D. $sin^{-1}\left(\frac{(x+2)}{(x-2)}\right)$

8. Which inequality defines the domain of the function f(x) = $\frac{1}{\sqrt{x+5}}$

   A. x > 5
   B. x > -5

C. x < 5
D. x < -5

Two straight roads meet at R at an angle 60degree. At time t = 0, car A leaves R on one road and car B is 100km from R on the other road. Car A travels away from R at a speed of 80 km/h and car B travels towards R at a speed of 50 km/h.

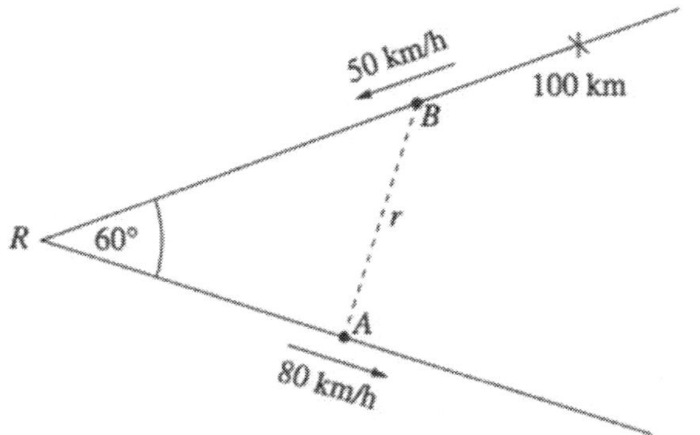

The distance between the cars at time t hours is r km.

9. Find r in terms of t

A. $\sqrt{12900t^2 - 18000t + 10000}$
B. $\sqrt{12900t^2 + 18000t - 10000}$
C. $\sqrt{12900t^2 - 18000t - 10000}$
D. $\sqrt{12900t^2 + 18000t + 10000}$

10. Which of the following is a root(s) of the equation $9x^3 - 4x = -18x^2 + 8$

A. 3/2
B. -2
C. -3/2
D. All of the above

11. Simplify the equation $\frac{x^2-2x-8}{x^2-9x+20}$

A. $\frac{x+2}{x-5}$

B. $\frac{x-2}{x+5}$

C. $\frac{x+4}{x-5}$

D. $\frac{x-4}{x+5}$

12. Simplify the equation $\frac{x^2-9}{x^2+5x+6} \div \frac{3-x}{x+2}$

A. x + 3
B. x - 3
C. -1
D. 1

For questions 13 and 14

In the diagram below, the sector BCD has center B and $\angle DBC = \frac{5\pi}{6}$.

The points A, B, and C lie on a straight line and AB = AD = 2 meters.

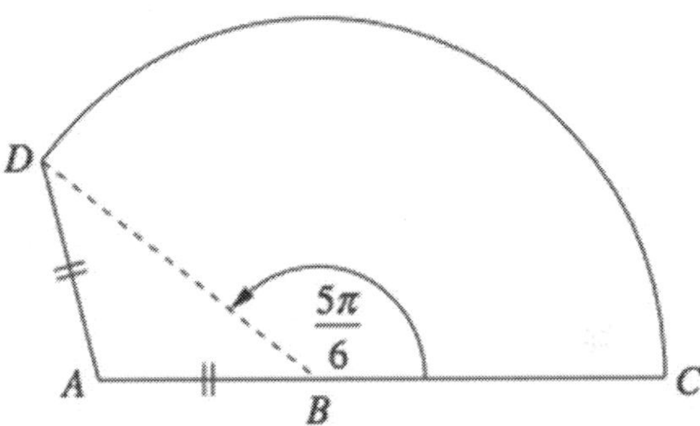

13. From the figure above, what is the $\angle DAB$?

A. $\frac{\pi}{3}$

B. $\frac{2\pi}{3}$

C. $\frac{\pi}{2}$

D. $\frac{2\pi}{5}$

14. What is $\frac{5\pi}{6}$ in degrees?

A. 150°
B. 30°
C. 180°
D. 32°

15. Simplify: $\frac{(4x^2y^{-2})^4}{(8xy^3)^4}$

A. $\frac{x^4}{16y^{20}}$

B. $\frac{x^4}{y^{20}}$

C. $\frac{x^4}{4y^{20}}$

D. $\frac{x^4}{16y^{-20}}$

Student-Produced Responses

16. The length of a rectangle is 30mm more than its width and the area is 400mm^2. Find the perimeter.

17. Solve $(67)^2 - (33)^2$

18. If $10^{2x} = 36$ then 10^{-x} equals:

19. For what value of the constant K does the equation 4x + Kx = 5 have one solution?

20. Find M so that the lines with equations -3x + My = 6 and 2y + x = -8 are perpendicular

No Test Material On This Page

Section 4

Math Test – Calculator
Allotted Time: 55 Minutes
Number of Questions: 38

Calculator **IS** allowed.

Reference Formulas

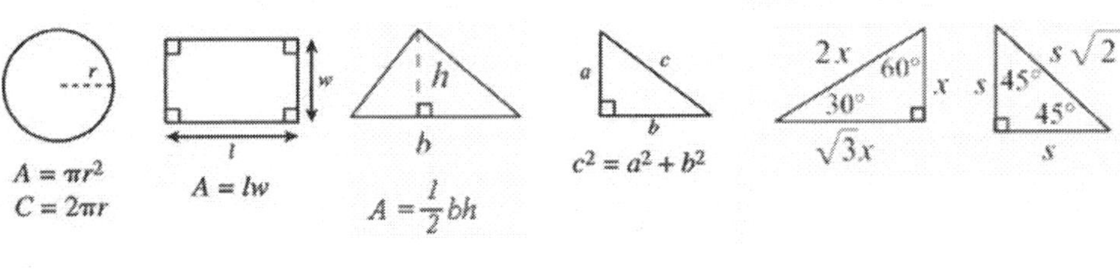

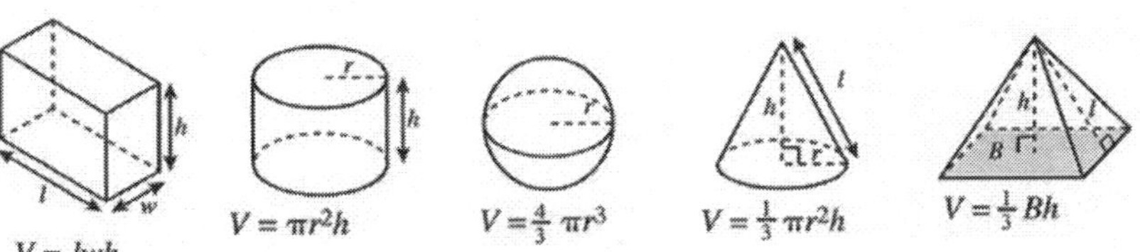

The number of degrees of arc in a circle is 360.
The number of radians of arc in a circle is 2π.
The sum of the measures in degrees of the angles of a triangle is 180.

21. If I just sold my two bags at $120 each, and on one I gained 20% and on the other I lost 20%, then:

A. I lost $20
B. I gain $20
C. I lost $10
D. I gain $30

22. It took John 20 minutes to sprint from point A to point B. On his way back to point A, he increased his speed by 40 meters per minute and it took him 12 minutes. What is his average speed for the whole journey?

A. 75
B. 90
C. 85
D. 100

23. The equation $x^2 + 5x - 2 = 0$ has roots α and β. What is the value of $\alpha\beta + (\alpha + \beta)$?

A. -4
B. -7
C. 7
D. -4

24. The square in the figure has all its vertices on the circle. The area of the square is 100. What is the area of the circle?

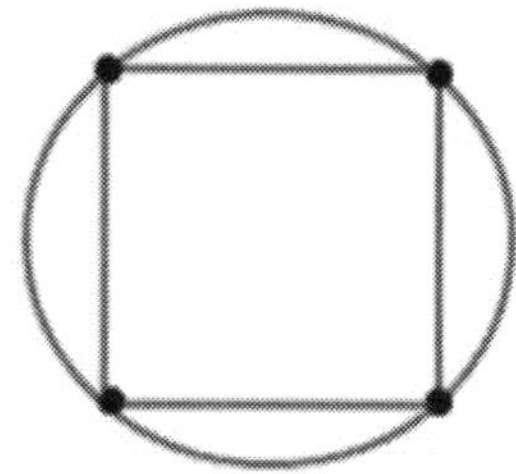

A. 162
B. 157
C. 145
D. 200

For questions 25 and 26:

A pack of 52 cards consists of four suits with 13 cards in each suit.

25. One card is drawn from the pack and kept on the table. A second card is drawn and placed beside it on the table. What is the probability that the 2nd card is from different suit to the first?

A. 0.65
B. 0.76
C. 0.86
D. 0.90

26. The two cards are replaced and the packed shuffled. 4 cards are chosen from the pack and placed side by side on the table. What is the probability that these 4 cards are all from different suits?

A. 0.105
B. 0.213
C. 0.053
D. 0.305

27. What is the perpendicular distance of the point (-2, 3) from the line y = 5x + 2?

A. $\frac{11}{\sqrt{26}}$

B. $\frac{21}{\sqrt{26}}$

C. $\frac{11}{\sqrt{25}}$

D. $\frac{21}{\sqrt{25}}$

28. The area of a sector of a circle of radius 4 cm is 60 cm^2. Find the length of the arc of the sector.

A. 25
B. 40
C. 35
D. 30

For questions 29 – 31

In a group of 50 people, 10 are healthy and every person of the remaining 40 has either high blood pressure, a high level of cholesterol or both. If 25 have high blood pressure and 35 have high level of cholesterol.

29. How many people have both high blood pressure and a high level of cholesterol?

A. 25
B. 20
C. 15
D. 10

30. If a person is selected randomly from this group, what is the probability that he or she has high blood pressure?

A. 0.3
B. 0.2
C. 0.6
D. 0.5

31. If a person is selected randomly from this group, what is the probability that he or she has high level of cholesterol

A. 0.7
B. 0.5
C. 0.9
D. 0.3

For questions 32 – 34

There are 12 donuts in a box. 4 donuts have caramel flavor, 4 have chocolate flavor and 4 have strawberry flavor. Liza randomly selects two donuts and eats them.

32. What is the probability that the 2 donuts have chocolate flavor?

A. 0.09
B. 0.12
C. 0.05
D. 0.14

33. What is the probability that the 2 donuts have the same flavor?

A. 0.21
B. 0.18
C. 0.27
D. 0.33

34. What is the probability that the 2 donuts have different flavor?

A. 0.79
B. 0.67
C. 0.73
D. 0.92

35. In a cafeteria, 3 teas and 4 biscuits cost \$10.05. In the same cafeteria, 5 teas and 7 biscuits cost \$17.15. How much do you have to pay for 4 teas and 6 biscuits?

A. Cannot be determined
B. \$13.50
C. \$14.20
D. \$15.60

36. For a given set of data, how will it affect the standard deviation if you add the value 5 to each term in the set?

A. Increase
B. Decrease
C. No change
D. Insufficient data

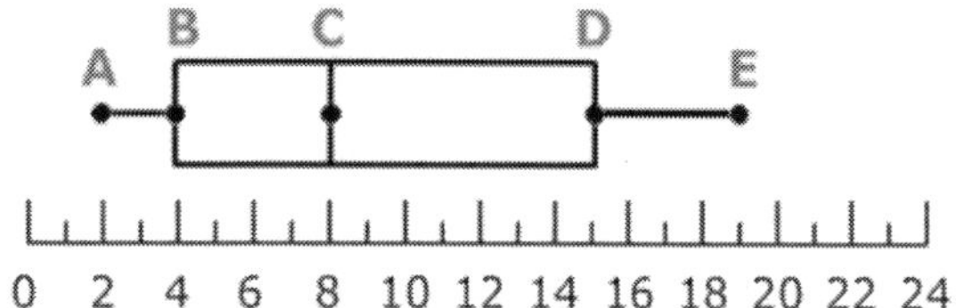

37. In the box-and-whisper plot above, what do the points B and D represent?

    A. The means of the first half of the data set and the second half of the data set, respectively.
    B. The medians of the first half of the data set, and the second half of the data set, respectively.
    C. The minimum and the maximum, respectively.
    D. The mean and the median, respectively.

For questions 38 – 40

Sam is making a pattern using triangular tiles. The pattern has 3 tiles in the first row, 5 tiles in the second row and each successive row has 2 more tiles than the previous row.

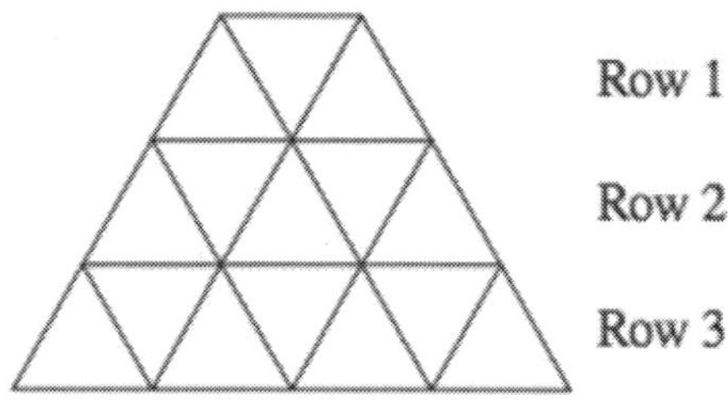

38. How many tiles would Sam use in row 15

    A. 30
    B. 31
    C. 32
    D. 33

39. How many tiles would Sam use altogether to make the first 15 rows?

    A. 255
    B. 275
    C. 300
    D. 305

40. Sam has only 200 tiles, how many complete rows of the pattern can Sam make?

    A. 10
    B. 15
    C. 13
    D. 20

41. Two resistors, when connected in series have a total resistance of 20 Ohms. If they are connected in parallel, the resistance is 5 Ohms. What are the resistor values?

    A. 10 Ohms each
    B. 20 Ohms each
    C. 10 Ohms and 20 Ohms
    D. 10 Ohms and 5 Ohms

42. In the diagram, the shaded region is bounded by the x-axis and the lines y = x and y = -2x+3. The area of the shaded region is?

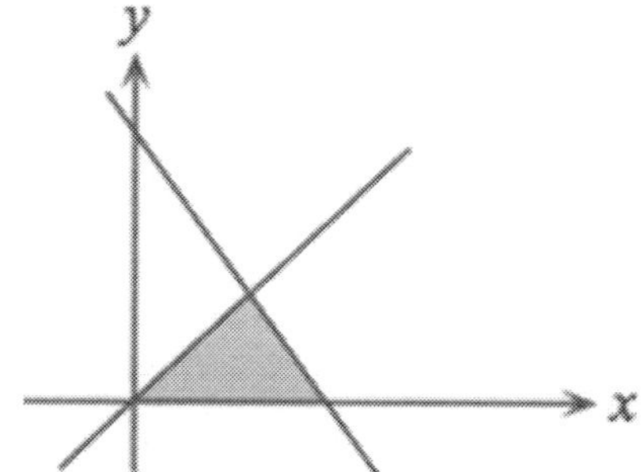

A. 1/4
B. 2/5
C. 3/4
D. 1/2

43. The velocity of a particle moving along the x-axis is given by x = 10 – 2t, where x is the displacement from the origin in meters and t is the time in seconds. Initially, the particle is 5 meters to the right of the origin. Find the time when the particle is at rest

A. 3 seconds
B. 4 seconds
C. 5 seconds
D. 6 seconds

Consider the following three data sets X, Y, and Z.

X = {8, 6, 9, 10, 12}
Y = {10, 12, 12, 13, 13}
Z = {1, 5, 9, 12, 8}

44. What is the mean of set Z?

A. 7
B. 6
C. 5
D. 10

45. The probability that John's basketball team wins this weekend is 1/5. The probability that Matt's baseball team wins this weekend is 2/3. What is the probability that neither teams wins this weekend?

A. 0.27
B. 0.34
C. 0.18
D. 0.22

46. Rank the following measures on how they are affected by outliers, in order from "least affected" to "most affected."

A. Mean, median, range
B. Median, mean, range
C. Range, median, mean
D. Median, range, mean

For questions 47 – 49

Weather records for a town suggest that:

- If a particular day is wet (W), the probability of the next day being dry is 5/6
- If a particular day is dry (D), the probability of the next day being dry is 1/2

In a specific week Thursday is dry. The tree diagram shows the possible outcomes for the next 3 days: Friday, Saturday and Sunday.

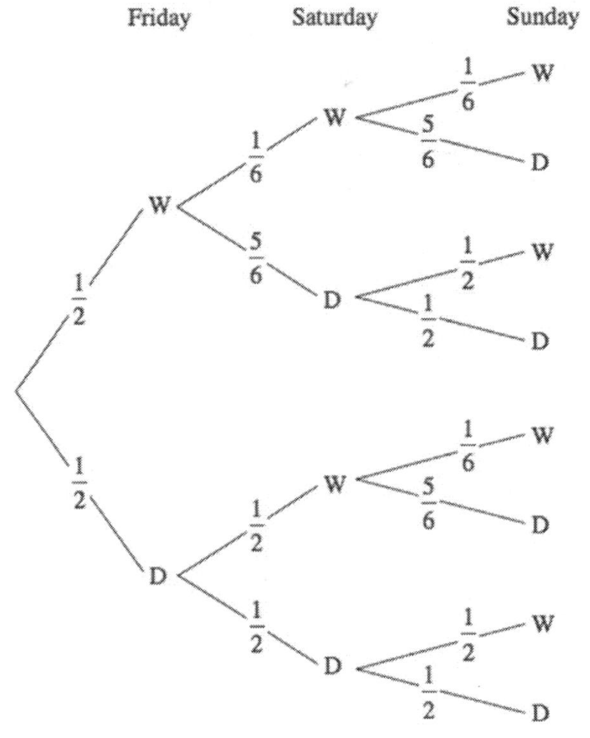

47. What is the probability that Saturday being wet?

    A. 0.67
    B. 0.25
    C. 0.75
    D. 0.33

48. What is the probability of both Saturday and Sunday being dry?

    A. 0.33
    B. 0.67
    C. 0.90
    D. 0.10

49. What is the probability of at least one of Saturday and Sunday being wet?

    A. 0.33
    B. 0.67
    C. 0.90
    D. 0.10

FISHING LICENSES SOLD IN METRO AREA BY COUNTY
= 1000 fishing licenses

County	
Beaufort County	
Clinton County	
Ingram County	
Hamilton County	
Lenawee County	

50. From the pictograph shown, what is the ratio of fishing licenses sold in Ingram County to Lenawee County?

    A. 9:5
    B. 5:9
    C. 5:11
    D. 1.5:45

Student-Produced Responses

51. Deepika can walk 3600 feet in 10 minutes. Walking at the same rate, how many yards can she walk in 10 seconds? (1 yard = 3 feet)

52. At St. John High School, 35% of the students are members of the Glee Club. 22% are members of both Glee and Cheer dance clubs. What is the probability that a student is a member of Cheer dance club if it is known that she is a member of the Glee club?

53. There are 40 students in a class and their results are presented as below:

Result (Pass/Fail)	Pass	Fail
Number of Students	25	15

If a student chosen randomly out of the class, Find the probability that the student has failed the examination? (Round your answer to two decimal places.)

54. A ball is thrown upwards from a rooftop, 80m above the ground. It will reach a maximum vertical height and then fall back to the ground. The height of the ball from the ground at time t is h which is given by $h = -16t^2 + 64t + 80$.

What is the height reached by the ball after 3 seconds?

55. What is the maximum height reached by the ball?

56. How long will it take before hitting the ground?

For questions 57 and 58

ABC is a triangle where AN is perpendicular to BC and BM is perpendicular to AC. The length BC is 5, that of AC is 6 and that of AN is 4.

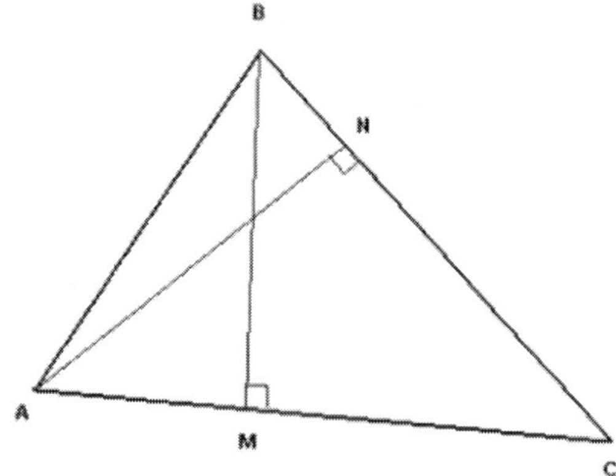

57. Find the length of BM

58. If MC = 4.5, find length AB

No Test Material On This Page

Test 2 Answer Key

#	Answer	#	Answer	#	Answer
1	B	21	C	41	A
2	A	22	A	42	A
3	B	23	B	43	C
4	C	24	B	44	A
5	C	25	A	45	A
6	C	26	A	46	B
7	A	27	A	47	D
8	B	28	D	48	A
9	A	29	B	49	B
10	D	30	D	50	B
11	A	31	A	51	20
12	C	32	A	52	0.63
13	B	33	C	53	0.38 OR 3/8
14	A	34	C	54	128
15	A	35	C	55	144
16	100	36	C	56	5
17	3400	37	B	57	10/3 OR 3.33
18	0.17 OR 1/6	38	B	58	3.65
19	-4	39	A		
20	1.5 OR 3/2	40	C		

TEST 3

ANSWER SHEET

Section 3

1 A B C D
2 A B C D
3 A B C D
4 A B C D
5 A B C D
6 A B C D
7 A B C D
8 A B C D
9 A B C D
10 A B C D
11 A B C D
12 A B C D
13 A B C D
14 A B C D
15 A B C D

16 17 18 19 20

/ . 0 1 2 3 4 5 6 7 8 9

Section 4

21 A B C D
22 A B C D
23 A B C D
24 A B C D
25 A B C D
26 A B C D
27 A B C D
28 A B C D
29 A B C D
30 A B C D
31 A B C D
32 A B C D
33 A B C D
34 A B C D
35 A B C D
36 A B C D
37 A B C D
38 A B C D
39 A B C D
40 A B C D
41 A B C D
42 A B C D
43 A B C D
44 A B C D
45 A B C D
46 A B C D
47 A B C D
48 A B C D
49 A B C D
50 A B C D

51

52

53

54

55

56

57

58

Section 3

Math Test – No Calculator
Allotted Time: 25 Minutes
Number of Questions: 20

Calculator **NOT** permitted.

Reference Formulas

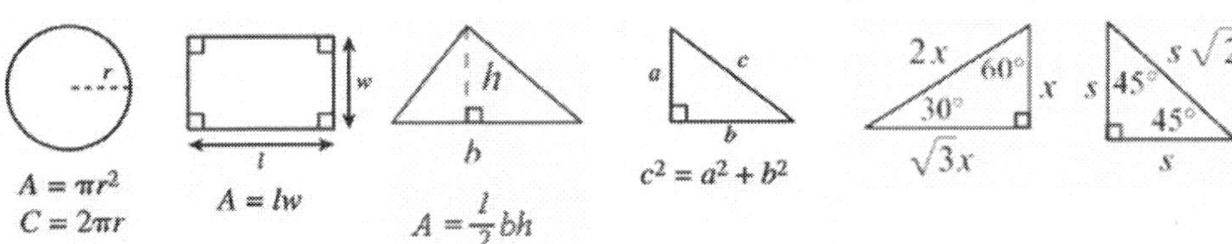

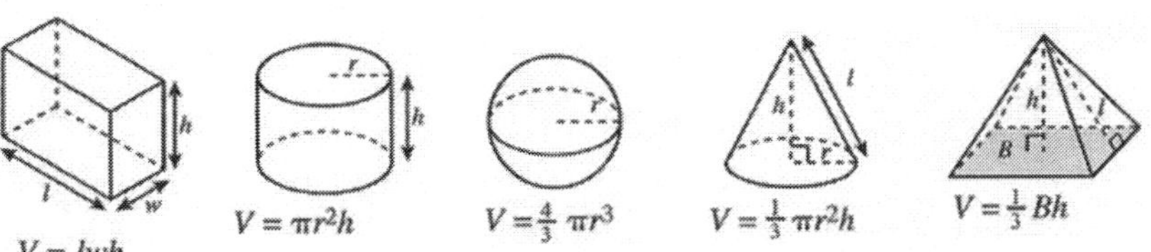

The number of degrees of arc in a circle is 360.
The number of radians of arc in a circle is 2π.
The sum of the measures in degrees of the angles of a triangle is 180.

1. If $3(x+k)-x=2k$ and $k=-1$, what is the value of $4-2x$?

A) -3
B) 3
C) -2
D) 2

2. For $i=\sqrt{-1}$, what is the product $(4+3i)(3-5i)$?

A) $12-15i^2$
B) $27-11i$
C) $12+15i$
D) $4-5i$

3. There are m cows and n chicken on the farm. Which of the following expressions represents the total number of their legs?

A) $m+n$
B) mn
C) $2(2m+n)$
D) $4mn$

4. The taxi driver charges start and every additional mile passed. The total cost C is represented by the equation $C=5+3n$. What is the meaning of value 5 in this equation?

A) The start of taxi drive costs \$5.
B) Every additional mile costs \$5.
C) First mile costs \$5.
D) Last mile costs \$5.

5.

$$(3x-2)(x^2+2x-1)$$

Which of the following is equivalent to the expression above?

A) $-3x^3+4x^2+7x-2$
B) $3x^3-4x^2-7x-2$
C) $3x^3+4x^2-7x+2$
D) $3x^3+4x^2-7x-2$

6.

$$P=100{,}000-34{,}000t$$

Sarah uses the model above to estimate the profit P of the company after t years. Based on the model, does the company make profit each year?

A) Yes
B) No
C) Yes, for the first 3 years
D) It is not possible to conclude

7.

$$F=\frac{GMm}{r^2}$$

The formula above gives the force of gravity F between two objects which masses are M and m and which are at distance r. Which of the following gives r in terms of F, G, M and m? (Note: G is gravitational constant 6.67×10^{-11})

A) $\sqrt{\frac{Mm}{FG}}$

B) $\sqrt{\frac{FmG}{M}}$

C) $\sqrt{\frac{Fm}{GM}}$

D) $\sqrt{\frac{GMm}{F}}$

8. If $2a+b=5$, what is the value of $\frac{a}{2b-10}$?

A) $\frac{1}{4}$

B) $\frac{1}{2}$

C) $-\frac{1}{4}$

D) $-\frac{1}{2}$

9.

$$4x - 5y = -23$$
$$3x + 2y = 0$$

What is the solution (x, y) to the system of linear equations above?

A) (-2,3)
B) (2,3)
C) (-2,-3)
D) (2,-3)

10.

$$f(x) = ax^2 - 3x + 2$$

For the function *f* defined above, *a* is a constant and *f*(3) = 2. What is the value of *f*(−3) ?

A) 14
B) 16
C) 18
D) 20

11.

$$m = 7 + 0.5h$$
$$n = 9 + 0.25h$$

In the equations above, *m* and *n* represent the temperature, in degrees Celsius, in two different cities, *h* hours after sunrise. After how many hours will the temperature in both cities be equal?

A) 7
B) 8
C) 9
D) 10

12. A line in the xy-plane passes through the origin. Which of the following points cannot lie on that line?

A) (-2,0)
B) (4,-2)
C) (-1,-3)
D) (2,5)

13. Which of the choices is equivalent to $\frac{1}{1-\frac{1}{x}}$?

A) $\frac{1}{1-x}$

B) $\frac{1}{x-1}$

C) $\frac{x}{x-1}$

D) $\frac{x}{1-x}$

14. If $2x - y = 4$, what is the value of $\frac{9^x}{3^y}$?

A) 3
B) 9
C) 27
D) 81

15. If $(ax + b)(2x - 1) = 10x^2 + cx - b$ for all values of x, and $a + b = 8$, what is the value of c?

A) 1
B) 2
C) 3
D) 4

Student-Produced Responses

16. If $x > 0$ and $x^2 - 5x - 24 = 0$, what is the value of x?

17. The sides of a triangle are 7, 3 and 6. The shortest side of a similar triangle is equal to the longest side of the triangle ABC. What is the longest side of the similar triangle?

18.

$$2x + 6 = 3y$$
$$\frac{y}{2} + 1 = x$$

What is the value of x in the system of equations above?

19. In a right triangle, one angle measures x^o, where $\cos x^o = \frac{5}{13}$. What is $\tan x^o$?

20. If $a = 4\sqrt{3}$ and $a\sqrt{3} = 2\sqrt{x}$, what is the value of x?

No Test Material On This Page

Section 4

Math Test – Calculator
Allotted Time: 55 Minutes
Number of Questions: 38

Calculator **IS** allowed.

Reference Formulas

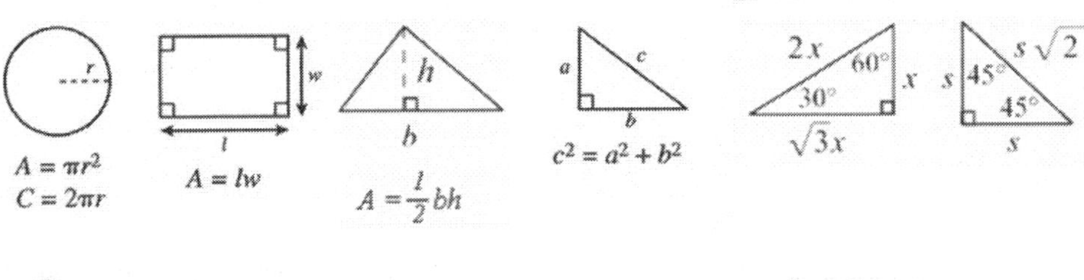

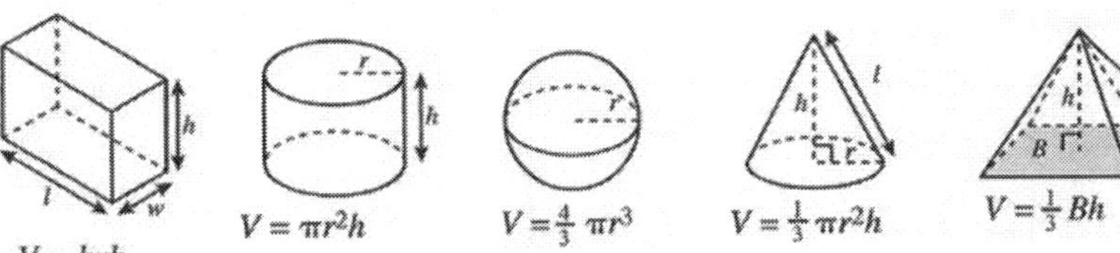

The number of degrees of arc in a circle is 360.
The number of radians of arc in a circle is 2π.
The sum of the measures in degrees of the angles of a triangle is 180.

21. The bus is traveling at different speeds. The graph below shows its speed at different times during journey. What is the average speed of the bus in the first 4 minutes?

A) 10
B) 20
C) 25
D) 30

22. A line passes through the point (12,-4) and intersects y-axis at 4. Which of the following points is the x-intercept of line?

A) (3,0)
B) (4,0)
C) (5,0)
D) (6,0)

23.

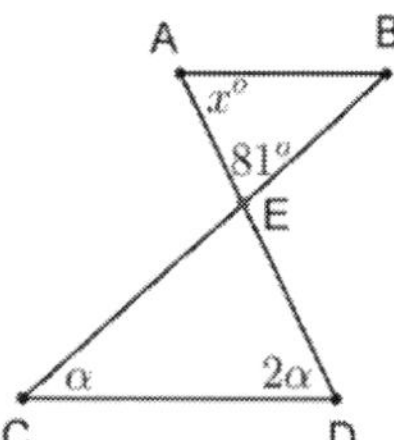

In the figure above, segments AB and CD are parallel. What is the measure of x^o?

A) 55°
B) 66°
C) 77°
D) 88°

24. If $\frac{3x-2}{4}$ is 2 less than 3, what is the value of $3-2x$?

A) 2
B) 1
C) -1
D) -2

25. Which of the following graphs shows a strong negative association between x and y?

A)

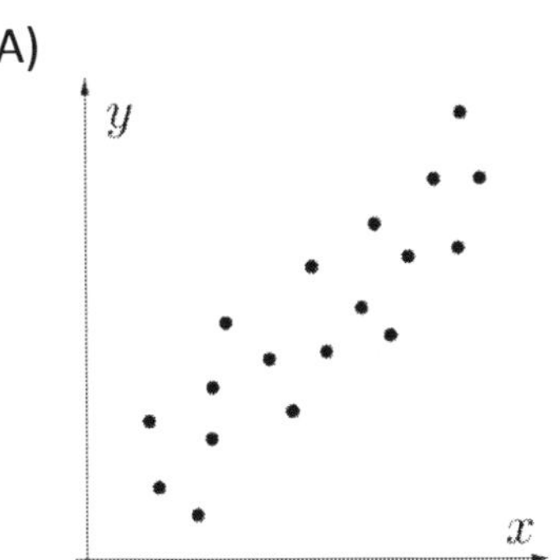

B)

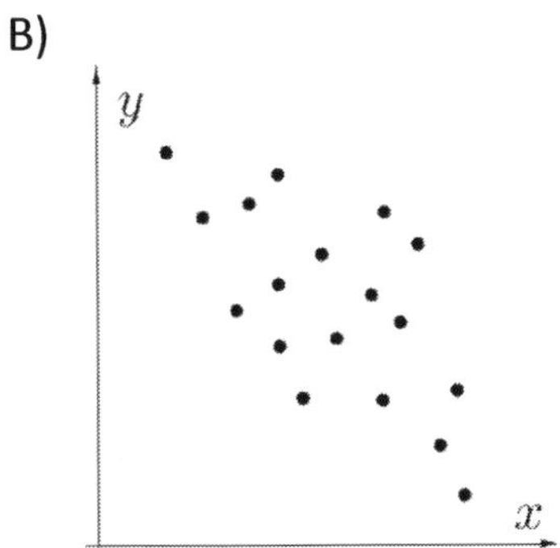

C)

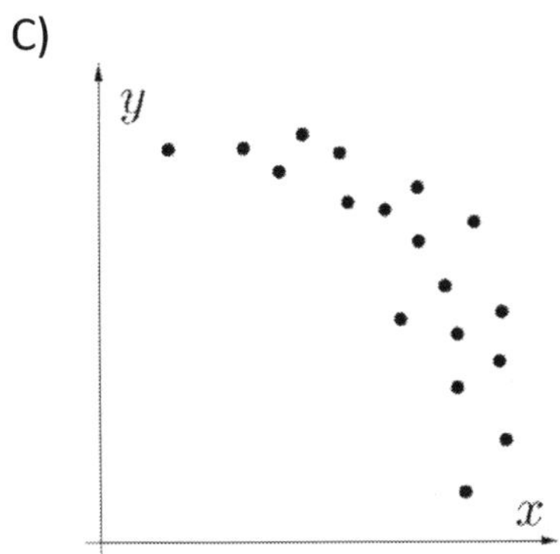

D)

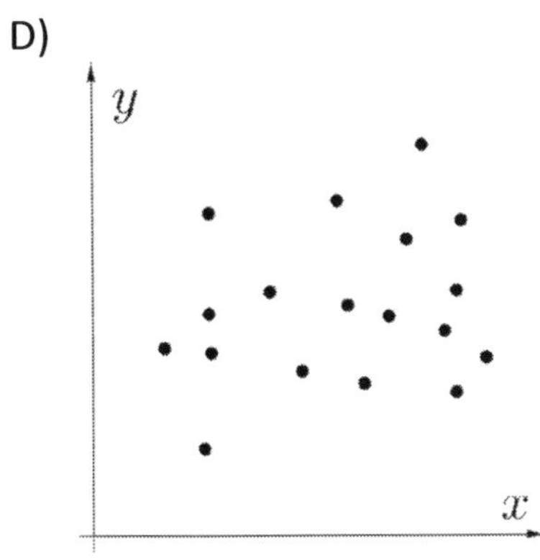

26. $1\ Gallon = 4\ quarts = 8\ pints = 16\ cups = 128\ fluid\ ounces$

How many cups can be poured with 3 quarts of juice?

A) 8
B) 10
C) 12
D) 14

27.

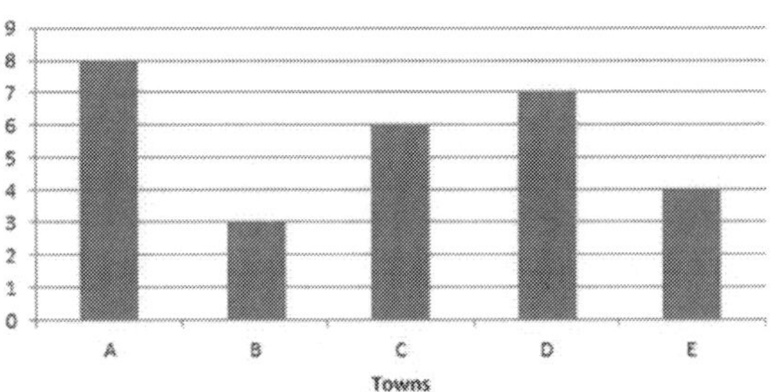

The number of citizens in 5 towns is shown in the graph above. If the sum of citizens in all 5 towns is 280,000, what is an appropriate label for the vertical axis of the graph?

A) Number of citizens (in hundreds)
B) Number of citizens (in thousands)
C) Number of citizens (in ten thousands)
D) Number of citizens (in hundred thousands)

28. If $|x-2|<3$, what are the possible values for x?

A) $1<x<5$
B) $-1<x<5$
C) $x<1$
D) $x<5$

Questions 29 and 30 refer to the following information.

$$P = \frac{20}{20 + R}$$

The probability *P* of picking a green apple, from the bag which contains 20 green and *R* red apples is shown in the formula above.

29. Which of the following expresses the number of red apples *R* in terms of the probability *P*?

A) $\frac{20P}{P-1}$
B) $\frac{20P}{1-P}$
C) $\frac{20(P-1)}{P}$
D) $\frac{20(1-P)}{P}$

30. How many red apples should be in a bag so that the probability of picking a red apple is 0.2?

A) 5
B) 6
C) 7
D) 8

31. Which of the following numbers is NOT a solution of the inequality $\frac{2x}{3} - 1 < \frac{1}{3} + \frac{x}{2}$?

A) 5
B) 6
C) 7
D) 8

32.

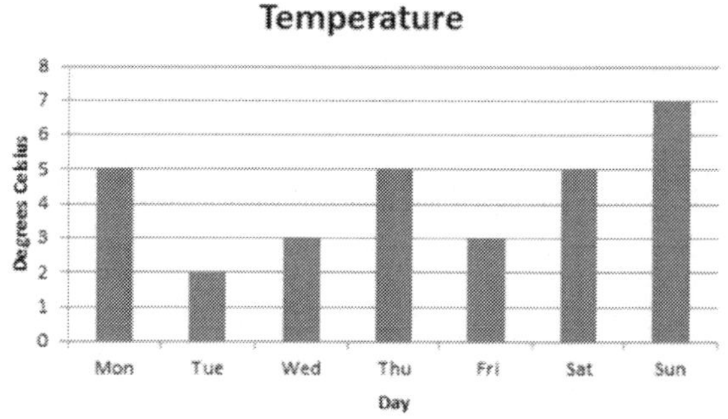

What is the median of the data in the graph above?

A) 3
B) 4
C) 5
D) 6

33.

		Pets			
		Dogs	Cats	Parrots	Total
Gender	Female	12	18	12	42
	Male	24	6	8	38
	Total	36	24	20	80

The table above shows the number of pets according to their gender. What is the percent of male cats among all cats?

A) 20%
B) 22.5%
C) 25%
D) 27.5%

34.

The number of shirts sold in April						
21	45	12	16	32	25	12
7	13	25	21	8	14	7
9	12	21	16	7	26	8
25	11	5	16	12	27	5

How much will range change if you omit the last row?

A) 1

B) 2
C) 3
D) 4

Questions 35 and 36 refer to the following information:

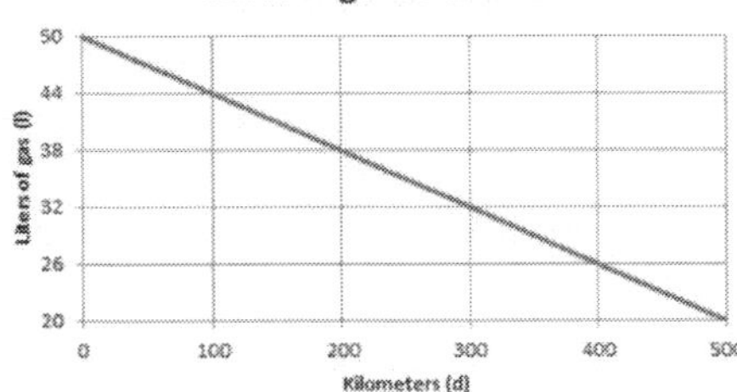

The graph above displays the level of gas in the tank *l*, in liters, depending on the distance passed *d*, in kilometers.

35. How many liters of gas is needed to pass 200 kilometers?

A) 3
B) 6
C) 9
D) 12

36. What is the level of gas in the tank after 350 kilometers?

A) 36
B) 35
C) 29
D) 28

37.

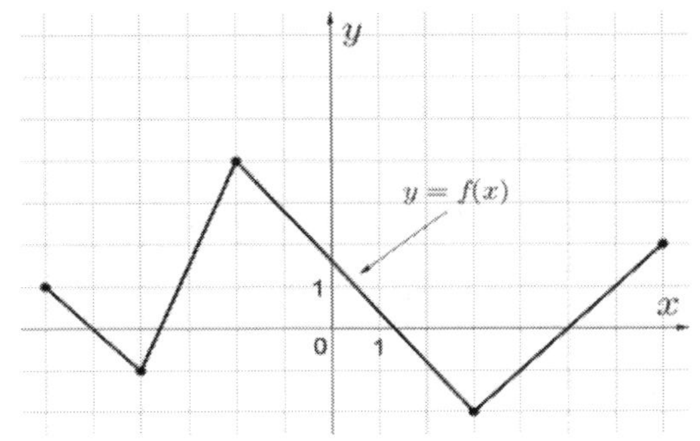

The graph of the function *f* is shown in the *xy*-plane above. What is the range of y?

A) $y < 4$
B) $y > -2$
C) $-2 < y < 4$
D) $-6 < y < 7$

38.

$$-2x > b + 3y$$
$$5x - a < 2y$$

If (1,-2) is the solution of the system of inequalities above, which of the following is true?

A) $a > b$
B) $a < b$
C) $|a + b| > b$
D) $|a + b| > a$

39. Noah bought 224 liters of coke for his birthday party. Coke is selling in bottles of 2 liters, and packs of 6 or 4 bottles. If he bought 21 packs of coke, how many 6-packs did he buy?

A) 7
B) 10
C) 14
D) 15

40. The price of a shirt increased 6%, and then decreased 4%. Emma bought a shirt for m dollars. Which expression shows the initial price of shirt in terms of m?

A) $\frac{1.06m}{0.96}$

B) $\frac{m}{1.06 \times 0.96}$

C) $\frac{0.96m}{1.06}$

D) $1.06 \times 0.96m$

41.

Years of experience of employees

	Less than 10	Between 10 and 20	Between 20 and 30	More than 30	Total
Males	12	14	8	6	40
Females	6	24	16	4	50
Total	18	38	24	10	90

The table above shows the number of employees based on their years of experience. If a person is chosen at random, what is the probability that it is female with more than 20 years of experience?

A) $\frac{1}{9}$
B) $\frac{2}{9}$
C) $\frac{1}{3}$
D) $\frac{4}{9}$

Questions 42 and 43 refer to the following information.

Number of students at Faculty of Natural Sciences and Mathematics

Department	Year			
	2010	2011	2012	2013
Math	120	90	110	86
Physics	86	90	96	108
Biology	94	76	88	92
Chemistry	108	120	115	103

The table above lists the number of students at Faculty of Natural Sciences and Mathematics from 2010 to 2013.

42. What is the average number of students at the Physics Department from 2010 to 2013?

A) 92
B) 93
C) 94
D) 95

43. What must be the number of students at the Chemistry Department in 2014, so that the average number of students from 2010 to 2014 would be 110?

A) 104
B) 106
C) 108
D) 110

44.

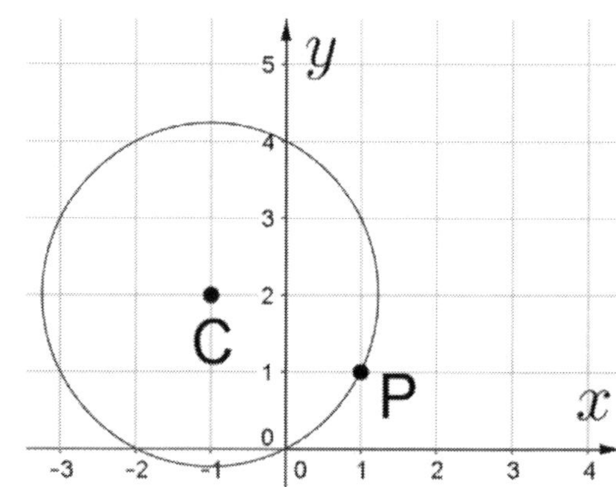

What is the equation of the circle in the graph above?

A) $(x-1)^2+(y+2)^2=5$
B) $(x+1)^2+(y-2)^2=5$
C) $(x-1)^2+(y+2)^2=3$
D) $(x+1)^2+(y-2)^2=3$

45.

$$P=\frac{1}{4}t^2+t-5$$

The profit P of the company, in millions of dollars, is given by the equation above, where t is time in years. At the end of which year did the company make loss of \$2,000,000?

A) 1st
B) 2nd

C) 3rd
D) 4th

46. There are 27 students in the class, where the number of boys is 25% greater than the number of girls. How many girls are there?

A) 12
B) 13
C) 14
D) 15

47. There are 8 grades in the school, with 4 classes in each grade, and 25 students in each class. A researcher randomly chose 5 classes and counted girls in each class.

Grade	2	4	5	7	8
Number of girls	8	5	12	7	18

What is the expected number of girls in the school?

A) 50
B) 120
C) 220
D) 320

48.

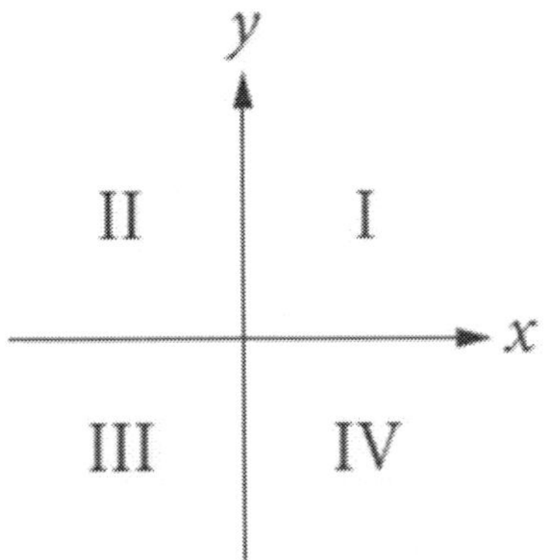

If the inequality $y \leq 3x + 5$ is graphed in the xy-plane above, all points in which quadrant are solutions to the inequality?

A) I
B) II
C) III
D) IV

49. If the remainder when a polynomial $a(x)$ is divided by $(x - 2)$ is 5, which of the following statements about $a(x)$ is true?

A) $a(2) - 5 = 0$
B) $a(-2) - 5 = 0$
C) $a(2) + 5 = 0$
D) $a(-2) + 5 = 0$

50. What is the equation of parabola which vertex is $V(1,4)$, and which intersects x-axis at $A(-1,0)$ and $B(3,0)$?

A) $y = -x^2 + 2x + 3$
B) $y = x^2 + 2x + 3$
C) $y = -x^2 + 2x - 3$
D) $y = x^2 - 2x + 3$

Student-Produced Responses

51. Alex is a math question writer. He creates at least 3, and at most 6 questions per hour. What is one possible number of hours he needs to create 12 questions?

52. If you subtract 18 from the positive integer, then divide by 3, and finally add 8, you will get the number greater than the starting number. What is one possible value for the starting number?

53.

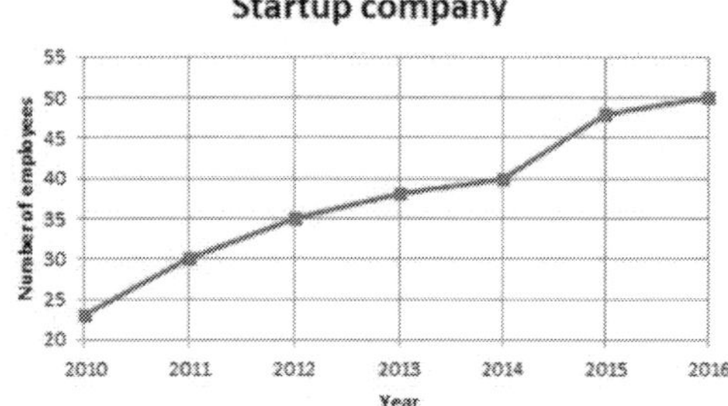

The number of employees in 2011 is what percent of the number of employees in 2014?

54. Mia works as a babysitter. She works at most 4 hours per day on weekday, and at most 2 hours per day on weekend. She charges $30 per hour on weekday, and $40 per hour on weekend. What is the maximum amount she can earn in one week?

55.

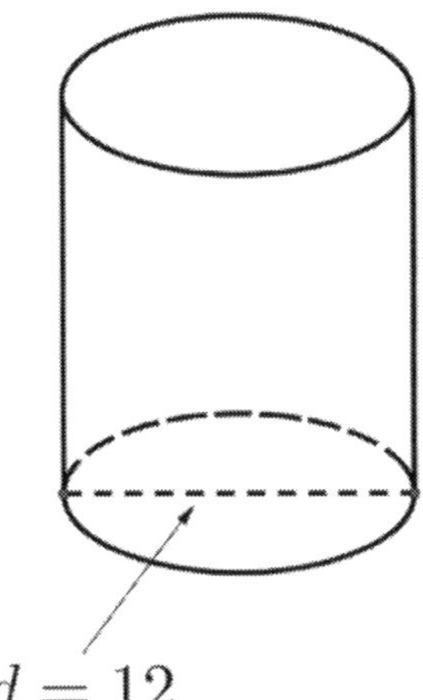

The gas tank is shown in the figure above. If its volume is 360π, what is its area? Round the final answer to nearest whole number. (Note: round π to 3.14)

56. What must be the value of k so that parabola $y = x^2 + 8x - 3k$ intersects x-axis in exactly one point?

Questions 57 and 58 refer to the following information.

The number of employees in the company falls 6% each year. In 2010, there were 2,200 employees. The expression $2{,}200 \times (x)^t$ is used to estimate the number of employees after t years.

57. What would be the value of x in the expression if the number of employees doesn't change?

58. After how many years will the number of employees be less than 2,000? (Round your answer to the whole number)

No Test Material On This Page

Test 3 Answer Key

#	Answer	#	Answer	#	Answer
1	B	21	B	41	B
2	B	22	D	42	D
3	C	23	B	43	A
4	A	24	C	44	B
5	C	25	B	45	B
6	B	26	C	46	A
7	D	27	C	47	D
8	C	28	B	48	D
9	A	29	D	49	A
10	D	30	A	50	A
11	B	31	D	51	2, 3, OR 4
12	A	32	C	52	1 OR 2
13	C	33	C	53	75
14	D	34	B	54	760
15	A	35	D	55	603
16	8	36	C	56	-5.3 OR -16/3
17	16.3 OR 49/3	37	C	57	1
18	3	38	A	58	2
19	2.4 OR 12/5	39	C		
20	36	40	B		

TEST 4

ANSWER SHEET

Section 3

1 A B C D	4 A B C D	7 A B C D	10 A B C D	13 A B C D
2 A B C D	5 A B C D	8 A B C D	11 A B C D	14 A B C D
3 A B C D	6 A B C D	9 A B C D	12 A B C D	15 A B C D

16	17	18	19	20
/	/	/	/	/
.	.	.	.	.
0	0	0	0	0
1	1	1	1	1
2	2	2	2	2
3	3	3	3	3
4	4	4	4	4
5	5	5	5	5
6	6	6	6	6
7	7	7	7	7
8	8	8	8	8
9	9	9	9	9

Section 4

21 A B C D	27 A B C D	33 A B C D	39 A B C D	45 A B C D
22 A B C D	28 A B C D	34 A B C D	40 A B C D	46 A B C D
23 A B C D	29 A B C D	35 A B C D	41 A B C D	47 A B C D
24 A B C D	30 A B C D	36 A B C D	42 A B C D	48 A B C D
25 A B C D	31 A B C D	37 A B C D	43 A B C D	49 A B C D
26 A B C D	32 A B C D	38 A B C D	44 A B C D	50 A B C D

51

52

53

54

55

56

57

58

Section 3

Math Test – No Calculator
Allotted Time: 25 Minutes
Number of Questions: 20

Calculator **NOT** permitted.

Reference Formulas

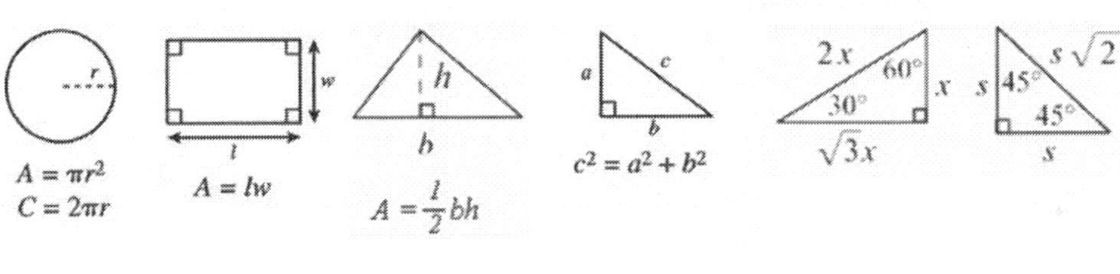

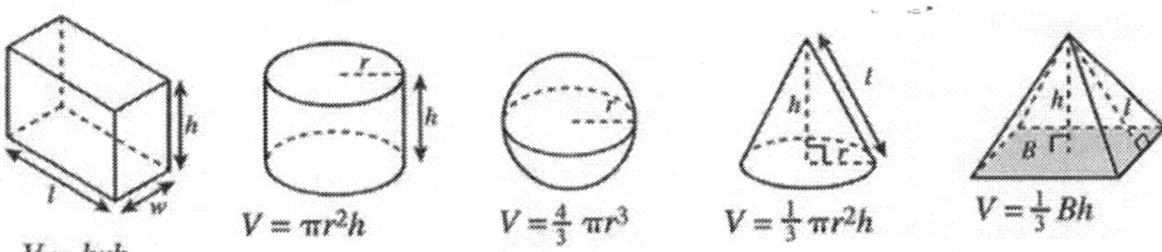

The number of degrees of arc in a circle is 360.
The number of radians of arc in a circle is 2π.
The sum of the measures in degrees of the angles of a triangle is 180.

1. If $x = 1, y = -\frac{3}{2}$ is a solution of the equation $3x + \alpha y = -3$, then α equals

A. 11
B. 4
C. 0
D. -1.5

2. The graph of a linear function and that of a quadratic function can intersect in

A. one, two or no points
B. at most three points
C. exactly two points
D. None of the above

3. A company pays its contractors by the formula $Pay = \$500 + K_c * Hours$. Here, $Hours$ represents the number of hours worked and K_c is a contractor specific constant. K_c of John is double that of Josh. If John and Josh work the same number of hours, then which of the following is true

A. John earns double that of Josh
B. John earns less than double that of Josh
C. John earns more than double that of Josh
D. None of the above

4. Which of the following is not true regarding the equation $x^2 + 5x + 4 = 0$

A. The sum of the roots is -5
B. -1 is a root of the equation
C. 4 is a root of the equation
D. The product of the roots is 4

5. Triangles ABC and PQR are similar. Triangle ABC is such that AB = 2BC. Which of the following must be true?

A. PQ = 2QR
B. PQ = AB
C. PR = 2PQ
D. None of the above

6. Originally, club X had 320 members. The club followed a policy wherein for each member leaving, two new members were inducted and new members were not accepted any other way. If n new members have been inducted till now, which of these is the correct expression for the size of the club?

A. 240
B. $320 + n$
C. $320 + \frac{n}{2}$
D. $320 - n$

7. $x = 5$ is a value that satisfies the equations $2x^2 - 9x + K = 0$ for an unknown constant K. The other value that satisfies the same equation is

A. -0.5
B. 9
C. $K/2$
D. 4

8. The number of solutions of the system of equations $x + 3y = 4$, $2x + y = 3$ and $x - y = 3$ is

A. one
B. two
C. infinity
D. zero

9. The function $q(x) = x^2 - 2x + 5$ is

A. always positive
B. takes both positive and negative values
C. always negative
D. takes all possible real values

10. The expression $\frac{x+3}{x+1} + \frac{x+1}{1-x}$ simplifies to

A. 4

B. $-\frac{4}{x^2-1}$

C. $\frac{2x+3}{x^2-1}$

D. $\frac{2x+3}{1-x^2}$

11. The function $m(x) = |x+1| + |1-2x|$. When $x > \frac{1}{2}$, m(x) equals

A. $|2-x|$
B. 2 - x
C. $3x$
D. $-3x$

12. The expression $\frac{1+i}{1-i} + \frac{1-i}{1+i}$ equals

A. 2
B. $2i$
C. 0
D. $-2i$

13. If $f(x)$ and $g(x)$ are polynomials such that $f(g(1)) = 0$ and $g(1) = 3.3$. Then which of the following is true?

A. 1 is a root of $f(x)$
B. 3.3 is a root of $g(x)$
C. 3.3 is a root of $f(x)$
D. 1 is a root of $g(x)$

14. Which of the following inequalities has a solution of length 3 units on the real line?

A. $|x+1| < 2$
B. $|2x-3| < 3$
C. $|5x-4| < 15$
D. $|x+1| > 3$

15. Let $q(x)$ be the quadratic function $q(x) = x^2 + 2x$. Then, $q(1) + q(\alpha) - 2q(\frac{1+\alpha}{2})$ is

A. zero
B. greater than zero
C. indeterminable
D. less than zero

Student-Produced Responses

16. For a triangle **Δ**ABC, the sides AB and AC are equal in length. If $angle\ BAC = 30°$, then $angle\ ACB$ is equal to?

17. What is the solution of the equation $120(\frac{3}{5} + \frac{4}{3}t) = 392$

18. In a village there are 300 more females than males. If the total population of the village is 6100, how many females are there in the village?

19. What is the coefficient of x in the product $(x+1)(x^2+4x+5)$?

20. For unknown values a and b, it is known that $2a+3b=7$. The value of the expression $4a^2+4a+9b^2+6b+12ab-5$ is?

No Test Material On This Page

Section 4

Math Test – Calculator
Allotted Time: 55 Minutes
Number of Questions: 38

Calculator **IS** allowed.

Reference Formulas

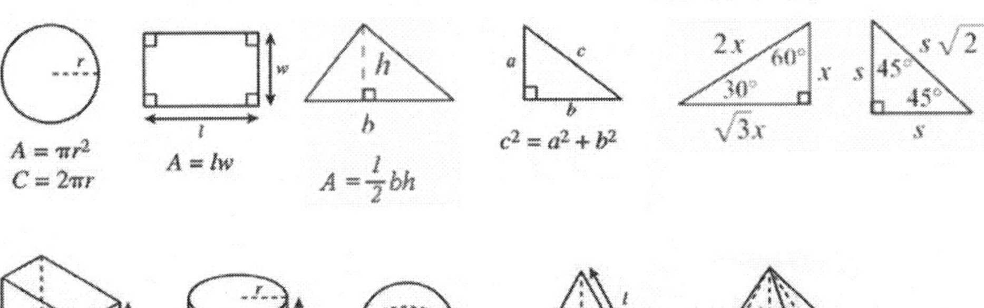

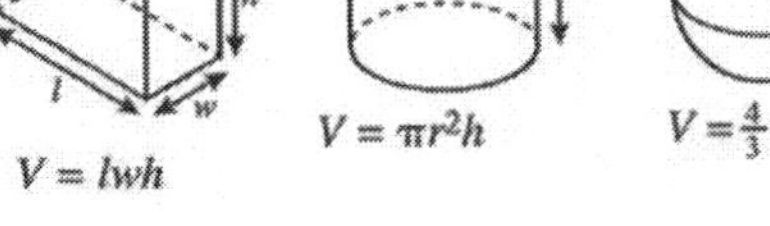

$V = \frac{4}{3}\pi r^3$

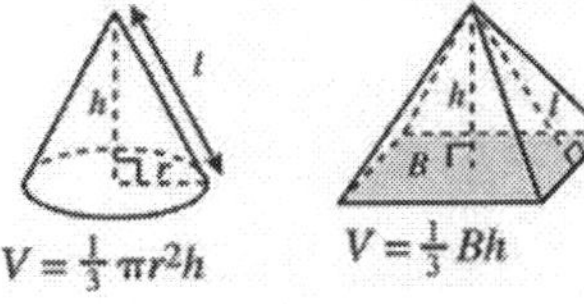

The number of degrees of arc in a circle is 360.
The number of radians of arc in a circle is 2π.
The sum of the measures in degrees of the angles of a triangle is 180.

For question 21 use the following graph that represents sales (in thousands) of a mobile app over a year.

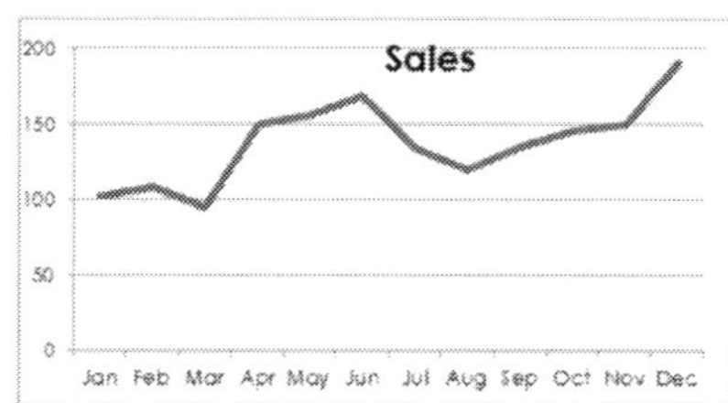

21. Which month had the lowest sales of the app?

A. January
B. April
C. August
D. March

22. Consider the function $h(x) = 3x + 7$. Compute $\frac{h(1+t)-h(1-t)}{2t}$

A. 3
B. 7
C. 4.5
D. 6

For questions 23 and 24 use the table given below. It records the results of a classification test on a randomized test group. The group was divided into two groups based on a well-defined criterion and then tested for inclusion in one of the types A, B or C.

	Type A	Type B	Type C
Group 1	14	24	35
Group 2	31	13	21

23. If a person, that was part of the test, is of Type A what is the probability that he is in Group 1?

A. $\frac{14}{45}$

B. $\frac{31}{45}$

C. $\frac{73}{138}$

D. $\frac{1}{2}$

24. If a person in Group 1 is not of Type A, what is the probability that he is of type C?

A. $\frac{35}{56}$

B. $\frac{35}{59}$

C. $\frac{56}{93}$

D. $\frac{56}{138}$

25. Find the largest integer x that satisfies the inequalities$x \leq 100 - 3y$ and $y > 0$

A. 100
B. 99
C. 97
D. 101

26. The set of equations $x + 2y = K$ and $4x = my + 12$ has infinitely many solutions. Then

A. $K = 3$ and $m = -8$
B. K = 12 and $m = 8$
C. $K = 3$ and $m = 8$
D. None of the above

For question 27, use the following graph of $f(x)$:

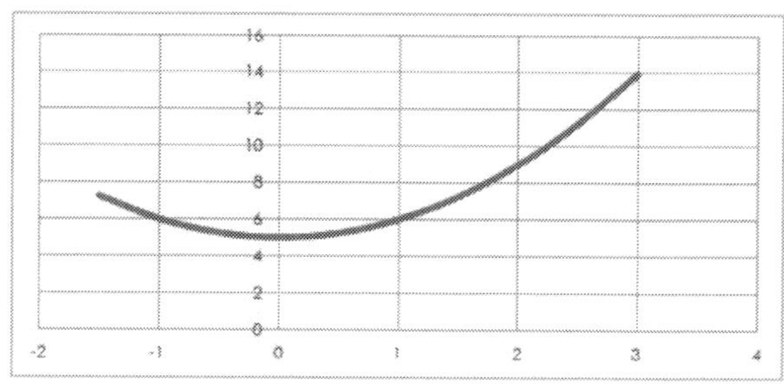

27. $f(x)$ is a quadratic polynomial whose graph is shown. Which of the following statements is incorrect?

A. $f(x)$ has a minimum at 0
B. $f(x) - 6$ has roots at 1 and -1
C. $f(x)$ has no real roots
D. $f(x) - 1$ has a root at 6

28. The quantity of diesel used by a car is directly proportional to the distance travelled. If a car has 50 liters of diesel, which of the following could represent the amount of diesel left after x miles?

A. $0.5x + 60$
B. $0.5x - 60$
C. $-0.5x + 60$
D. $-0.5(60x)$

29. Solve the system:

$$y + 3x = 2$$
$$x + y \geq 7$$

A. $x \leq -1/2$
B. $x \leq -5/2$
C. $-1 \leq x < 1$
D. $x \geq -5/2$

30. It is known that less dense liquids float over denser ones. Liquid A has density $5g/cm^3$. $10\ cm^3$ of liquid B weighs 35g and $14\ cm^3$ of liquid C weighs 40g. If the liquids are poured in a container, the order in which the liquids settle from top to bottom is

A. A above B above C
B. A above C above B
C. B above C above A
D. C above B above A

31. It is known that the equation $q(x)(x^2 - 1) = x^5 - ax + b$ holds for all x. Here, $q(x)$ is a polynomial and a and b are constants. Find the values of a and b.

A. a = 1, b = 2
B. a = 1, b = 0
C. a = 1, b = -1
D. None of the above

32. Heidi has to be at work at 9a.m. If she starts at 8 a.m. and walked to the station, she reaches right on time to take the 8:15 a.m. train. If, however, she started later at 8:05 a.m. she bikes to the next station about 3 miles farther and reaches there at 8:17 a.m. If her biking speed is 4.5 times her walking speed, how fast does she walk?

A. A mile in 10 minutes
B. A mile in 13 minutes
C. A mile in 15 minutes
D. A mile in 17 minutes

33. Which of the following statements is correct about the product of linear functions?

A. The product of two linear functions is quadratic
B. The product of two linear functions is linear
C. The product of any number of linear functions is always linear
D. The product of two linear functions may be cubic

34. How many values of x satisfy the equation $x + \sqrt{x+1} = 1$?

A. 0
B. 1
C. 2
D. 3

35. Mr. Dollmaker has created a number of dolls for an event. He has a limited amount of cloth. If he made pants, he will have enough pants for all the dolls and $5\ cm^2$ of cloth left. If he, instead, made shirts, then he would have a shortage of cloth for 3 dolls. If pants need $6\ cm^2$ of cloth and shirts need $7\ cm^2$ of cloth, how many dolls does he have?

    A. 35
    B. 33
    C. 24
    D. 26

For question 36 and 37 use the following bar graph that represents sales (in thousands) of three different products.

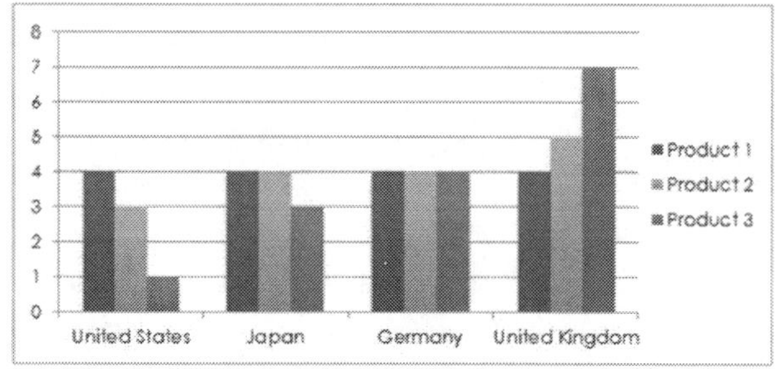

36. Which product has a better average sale among the countries shown? Pick the best answer.

    A. Product 1
    B. Product 2
    C. Product 3
    D. Product 1 and product 2

37. The sales of which product has the greatest standard deviation among the countries shown?

    A. Product 1
    B. Product 2
    C. Product 3
    D. All of the above

38. VinvestURmoney Company has two investment plans – A and B. Plan A provides an interest rate of 2.5% compounded quarterly. Plan B provides an interest rate of 4% compounded half-yearly. Over a period of 5 years, which of the two plans has better performance

    A. Plan A
    B. Pan B
    C. Cannot be determined
    D. None of the above

39. Dealer X marks up his goods by 30% and then provides his customers a discount of 10%. Dealer Y marks up his goods be 35% and on that price provides a discount of 15%. For the same good, which dealer's goods are more expensive?

    A. X
    B. Y
    C. Could be X or Y depending on the actual price of good
    D. None of the above

40. A chemist has two measuring cups, one shaped like a cone and the other shaped like a cylinder. They have the same base radius as well as equal height. If the chemist fills the cone with water and pours it fully into the cylinder (which is empty), what would the height of the water in the cylinder be?

    A. One-third of the height of the cylinder
    B. One-half of the height of the cylinder
    C. Two-third of the height of the cylinder
    D. A quarter of the height of the cylinder

41. The shaded region on the graph is defined by which of the following system of inequalities?

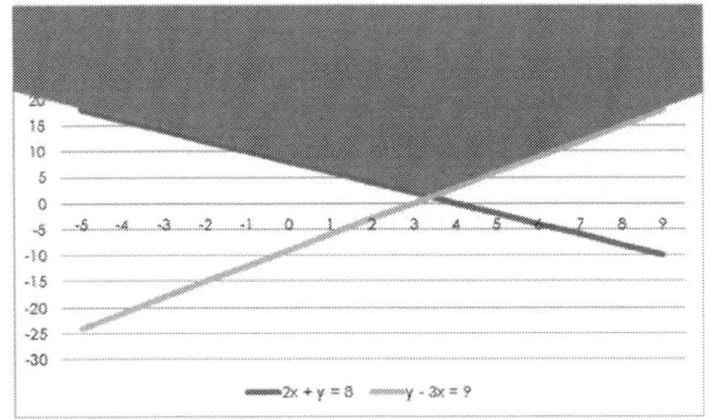

A. $2x + y \geq 8$ and $y - 3x \geq -9$
B. $2x + y \leq 8$ and $y - 3x \geq -9$
C. $2x + y \geq 8$ or $y - 3x \geq -9$
D. $2x + y \leq 8$ or $y - 3x \leq -9$

42. Hooke's law is a physical principle that states that the force F needed to extend a spring by a distance x is proportional to that distance. This is written as $F = Kx$ for a constant K that is a characteristic of the spring. Which of the following statements is correct about the constant K?

A. K is the amount of extension of the spring for one unit of force
B. For every unit increase in spring extension, K units of force are required
C. K is the same for all springs
D. K depends on x

43. Mr. A runs at a constant speed of 8 miles per hour. Mr. B runs at bursts of 10 miles per hour for two miles followed by a leisurely 7 miles per hour for one mile. Over a distance of 100 miles, who has the higher average speed?

A. Mr. A
B. Mr. B
C. Cannot be decided based on the information
D. None of the above

44. To double the area of a circle, the radius has to be increased by

A. 10%
B. 32.1%
C. 100%
D. 41.4%

The price of apples has fluctuated a lot recently. This is of special concern for Tom who eats an apple every day. Looking at the graph below, answer **questions 45 and 46**.

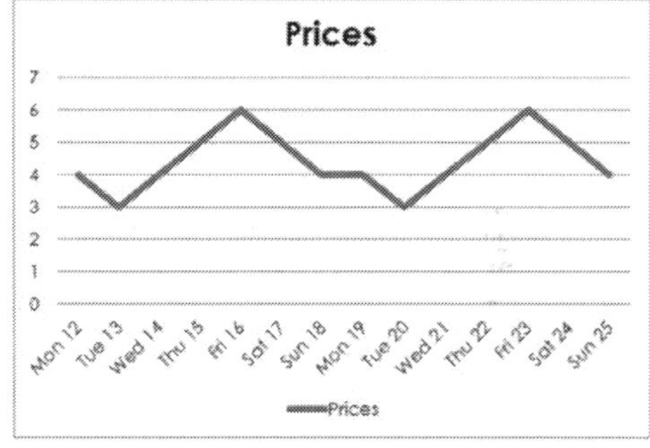

45. In the week 12 - 18, when was the price of apple the highest?

A. Tuesday
B. Thursday
C. Friday
D. Monday

46. Tom decides to buy apples for the whole week on one day of the week. Which day of the week would provide the maximum saving?

A. Sunday
B. Friday
C. Tuesday
D. Wednesday

For questions 47 and 48, use the table given below. The table records the ages of the students in a class.

Age	11	12	13	14
Number of students	3	14	9	8

47. What is the median age of the class?

   A. 12
   B. 13
   C. 12.5
   D. 11.5

48. If another student joins the class the median age would:

   A. Increase
   B. Decrease
   C. Remain the same
   D. None of the above

49. A right triangle has two sides of length 3 and 4 units. Which of the following could be length of the other side?

   A. 5.2
   B. $\sqrt{7}$
   C. $\sqrt{5}$
   D. 2

50. Lulu is participating in a five day run where each day she would run a distance of 10 miles. She wants to complete the entire event at an average speed of 50 miles per hour. Further, she wants to pace her speed so that starting from the first day her speed increase by 10% everyday till the third day of the week after which she decreases her speed by 10% till the final day. What is the speed with which she finishes the race?

   A. 53 miles per hour
   B. 50 miles per hour
   C. 45 miles per hour
   D. 37 miles per hour

Student-Produced Responses

51. The mean weight of a group of 9 kids is 70 lbs. If a new kid, whose weight is 65lbs, joins the group, what is the new mean? (state your answer up to one decimal place)

52. Skyler has only quarters and dimes in his pocket. He has 4 more dimes than he has quarters. If the total money he has is $4.25, how many quarters does he have?

53. For $(1 + 3i)(c + 4i)$ to be a real number, c should be

54. What is the slope of the line?

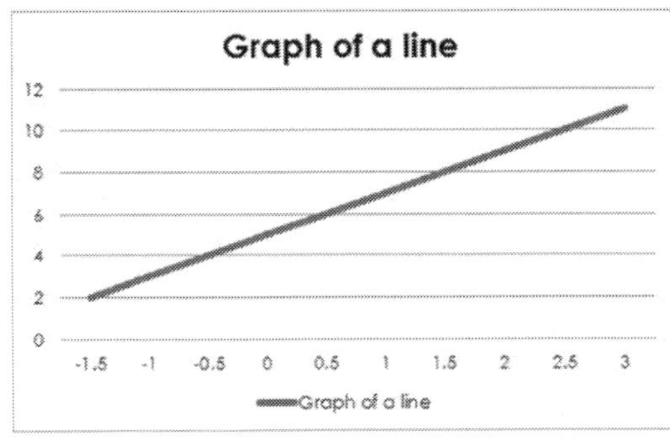

55. Half of all the fruits in a basket are apples. 20% of the apples are green apples. If there are exactly two green apples in the basket, how many fruits does the basket contain?

56. If a and b are real numbers such that $a + b = 4$ and $ab = 3$. Then $|a - b|$ is

57. Archimedes' principle states that the weight of liquid displaced by a floating object is equal to the weight of the object. A $30cm^3$ cubic block of wood of unknown density is dropped in a bucket of water and the wood floats displacing $20cm^3$ of water. What is the ratio of the density of the wood to that of water?

58. The last digit in the expansion of 2^{375} is?

No Test Material On This Page

Test 4 Answer Key

1	B	21	D	41	A
2	A	22	A	42	B
3	B	23	A	43	B
4	C	24	B	44	D
5	A	25	B	45	C
6	C	26	A	46	C
7	A	27	D	47	C
8	D	28	C	48	D
9	A	29	B	49	B
10	B	30	D	50	D
11	C	31	B	51	69.5
12	C	32	B	52	11
13	C	33	A	53	-1.3 OR -4/3
14	B	34	B	54	2
15	B	35	D	55	20
16	75	36	D	56	+2 OR -2
17	2	37	C	57	0.67 OR 2/3
18	3200	38	A	58	8
19	9	39	A		
20	58	40	A		

TEST 5

ANSWER SHEET

Section 3

1 A B C D
2 A B C D
3 A B C D
4 A B C D
5 A B C D
6 A B C D
7 A B C D
8 A B C D
9 A B C D
10 A B C D
11 A B C D
12 A B C D
13 A B C D
14 A B C D
15 A B C D

16 / . 0 1 2 3 4 5 6 7 8 9
17 / . 0 1 2 3 4 5 6 7 8 9
18 / . 0 1 2 3 4 5 6 7 8 9
19 / . 0 1 2 3 4 5 6 7 8 9
20 / . 0 1 2 3 4 5 6 7 8 9

Section 4

21 A B C D
22 A B C D
23 A B C D
24 A B C D
25 A B C D
26 A B C D
27 A B C D
28 A B C D
29 A B C D
30 A B C D
31 A B C D
32 A B C D
33 A B C D
34 A B C D
35 A B C D
36 A B C D
37 A B C D
38 A B C D
39 A B C D
40 A B C D
41 A B C D
42 A B C D
43 A B C D
44 A B C D
45 A B C D
46 A B C D
47 A B C D
48 A B C D
49 A B C D
50 A B C D

51

52

53

54

55

56

57

58

Section 3

Math Test – No Calculator
Allotted Time: 25 Minutes
Number of Questions: 20

Calculator **NOT** permitted.

Reference Formulas

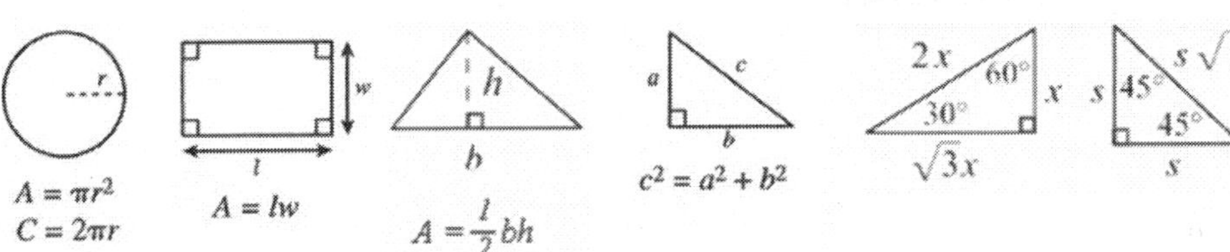

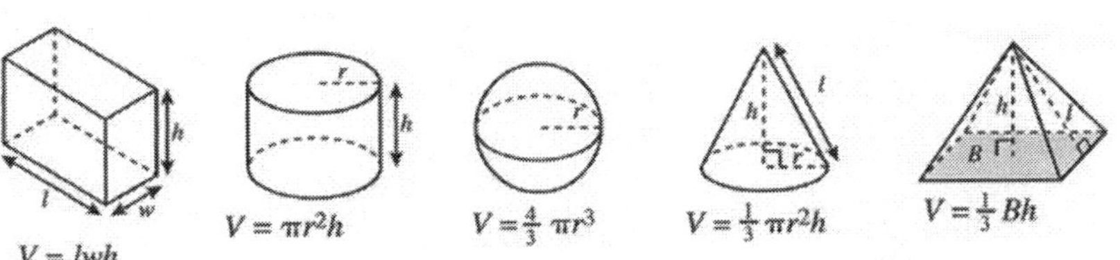

The number of degrees of arc in a circle is 360.
The number of radians of arc in a circle is 2π.
The sum of the measures in degrees of the angles of a triangle is 180.

1. If $x - 5 = k$ and $k = -2$, what is the value of $5x + 2$?

A) -7
B) 7
C) -17
D) 17

2. For $i = \sqrt{-1}$, what is the difference $(3 - 4i) - (1 + 7i)$?

A) $2 - 11i$
B) $2 + 3i$
C) $4 + 3i$
D) $4 + 11i$

3. The grocery store is opened t hours every day, except on Saturday, when it is opened k hours. The grocery store is closed on Sunday. Which of the following expressions represents the total number of hours during the week when the grocery store is opened?

A) $5t + k$
B) $7kt$
C) $6 + k + t$
D) $6kt$

4. Noah works as a salesman. His monthly salary is $\$m$, and he is paid $\$n$ for every item he sells. If he sold t items this month, which of the following expressions represents his total monthly earnings?

A) $30mn$
B) $m + 30n$
C) mnt
D) $m + nt$

5.

$$(4x^2 - 3x + 6) - (-2x^2 + 5x - 3)$$

Which of the following is equivalent to the expression above?

A) $2x^2 + 2x + 3$
B) $6x^2 - 8x + 9$
C) $-8x^4 - 15x^2 - 18$
D) $-6x^2 + 8x + 3$

6.

$$w = 96 - 2m$$

Emma uses the model above to estimate her weight w, after m months. Based on the model, what is her initial weight?

A) 96
B) 93
C) 48
D) 2

7.

$$F = \frac{GMm}{r^2}$$

The formula above gives the force of gravity *F* between two objects which masses are *M* and *m* and which are at distance *r*. Which of the following gives *m* in terms of *F*, *G*, *M* and *r* ? (Note: G is gravitational constant 6.67×10^{-11})

A) $\frac{Fr^2M}{G}$
B) $\frac{Fr^2G}{M}$
C) $\frac{Fr^2}{GM}$
D) $\frac{F}{r^2GM}$

8. If $a - 2b = -4$, what is the value of $\frac{a+2}{a+2b}$?

A) $\frac{1}{4}$

B) $\frac{1}{2}$
C) 1
D) 2

9.

$$x + y = -4$$
$$x - y = 6$$

What is the solution (x, y) to the system of linear equations above?

A) (1,-5)
B) (1,5)
C) (-1,-5)
D) (-1,5)

10.

$$f(x) = 3x - a$$

For the function *f* defined above, *a* is a constant and *f*(2) = 4. What is the value of *f*(−2) ?

A) -10
B) -8
C) -6
D) -4

11.

$$h = 25.5 + 3.5t$$

In the equation above, *h* represents the height of the balloon, in yards, after *t* seconds. After how many seconds will the balloon be at the height of 50 yards?

A) 7
B) 8
C) 9
D) 10

12. A line in the xy-plane is parallel to the x-axis and passes through the point (2,3). Which of the following points lies on the line?

A) (2,4)
B) (3,2)
C) (-1,3)
D) (1,-4)

13. Which of the following is equivalent to $\frac{1}{x} - \frac{1}{x-1}$?

A) $\frac{1}{x(1-x)}$
B) $\frac{1}{x(x-1)}$
C) $\frac{1}{1-x}$
D) $\frac{1}{x-1}$

14. If $x + y = 3$, what is the value of $2^x 2^y$?

A) 2
B) 4
C) 6
D) 8

15. If $(ax + 4)(2x + 5) = 6x^2 + bx + 20$ for all values of x, what is the value of b?

A) 13
B) 18
C) 23
D) 28

Student-Produced Responses

16. If $p < 0$ and $p^2 - 16 = 0$, what is the value of p?

17.

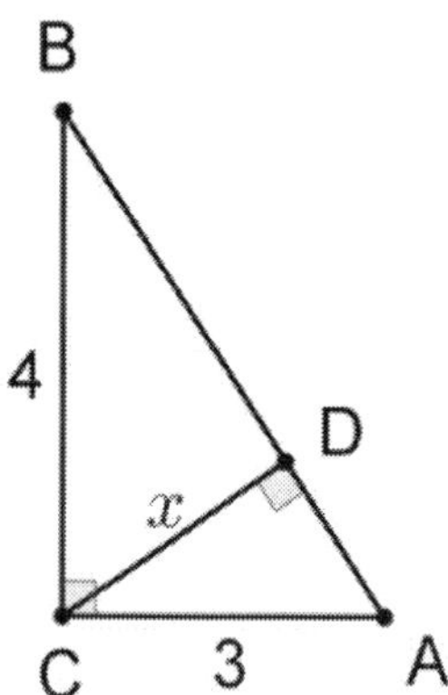

What is the length of x, in the triangle above?

18.

$$x - 2y = -4$$
$$x + 3y = 1$$

What is the value of x in the system of equations above?

19. In a right triangle, one angle measures x^o, where $\sin x^o = \frac{3}{5}$. What is $\cos x^o$?

20. What is the value of $\sqrt{12} - \sqrt{75} + \sqrt{27}$?

No Test Material On This Page

Section 4

Math Test – Calculator
Allotted Time: 55 Minutes
Number of Questions: 38

Calculator **IS** allowed.

Reference Formulas

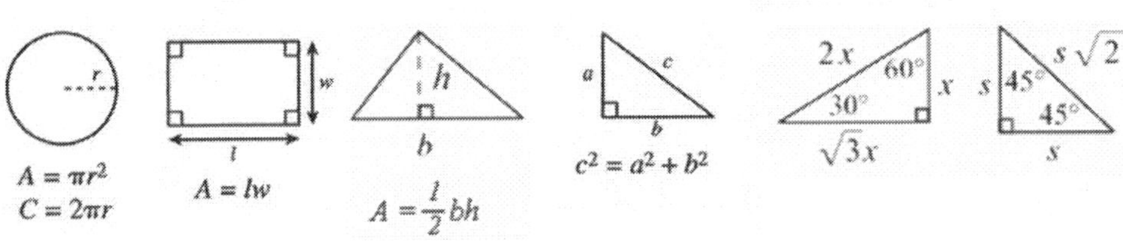

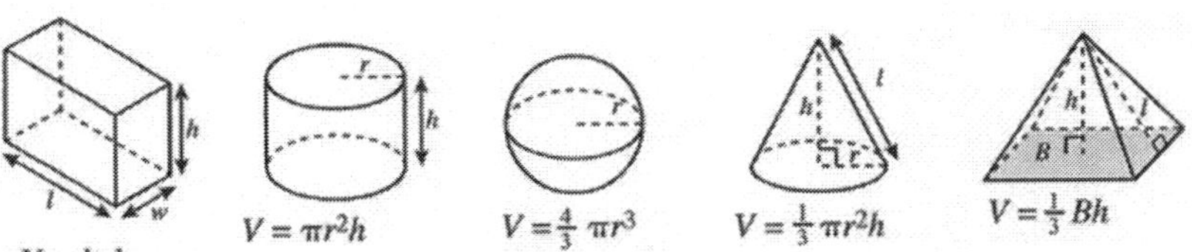

The number of degrees of arc in a circle is 360.
The number of radians of arc in a circle is 2π.
The sum of the measures in degrees of the angles of a triangle is 180.

21. The bus is traveling at different speeds. The graph below shows its speed at different times during journey. How many minutes does the bus travel at the constant speed?

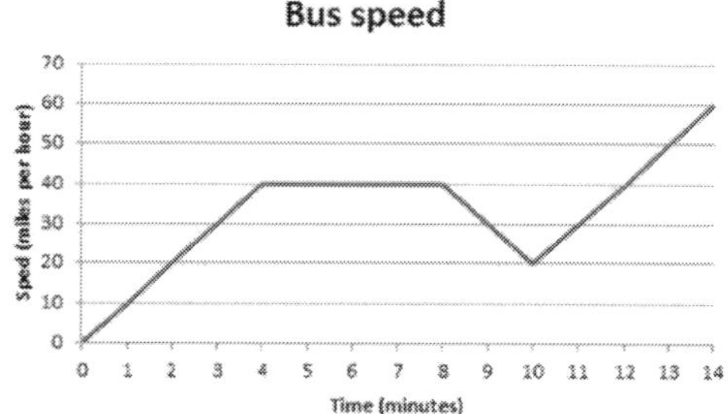

A) 2
B) 4
C) 6
D) 14

22. If line passes through the origin, and point (3,-5) lies on that line, what is the y-coordinate of the point (-6,y) which also lies on that line?

A) -3
B) 5
C) 6
D) 10

23.

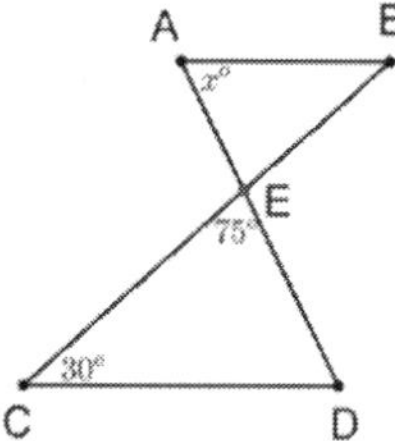

In the figure above, segments AB and CD are parallel. What is the measure of x^o?

A) 65°
B) 70°
C) 75°
D) 80°

24. If $4x - 5$ is 9 less than 12, what is the value of $2x$?

A) 2
B) 4
C) 6
D) 8

25. Which of the following graphs shows a positive association between x and y?

A)

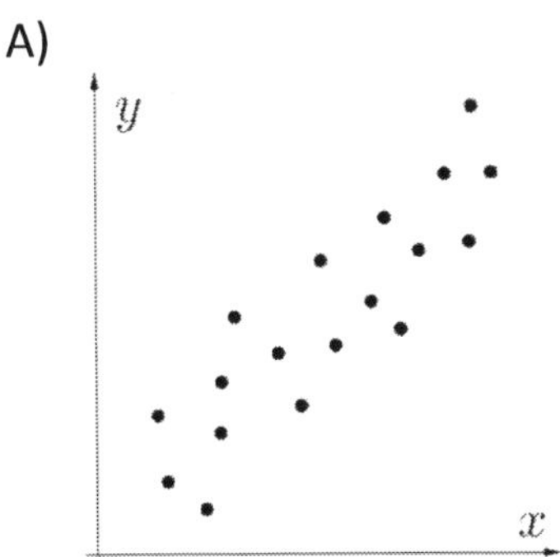

B)

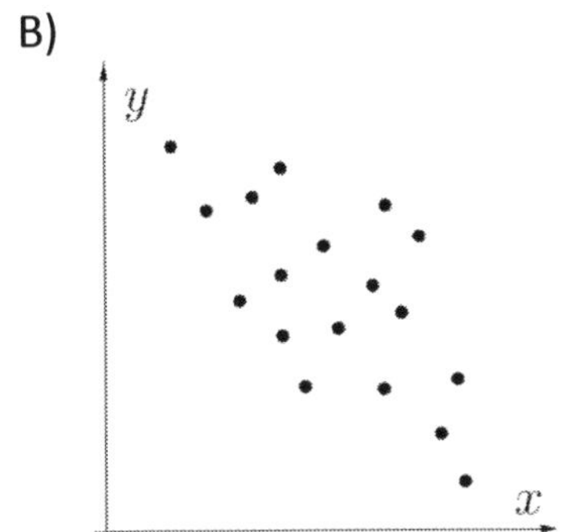

C)

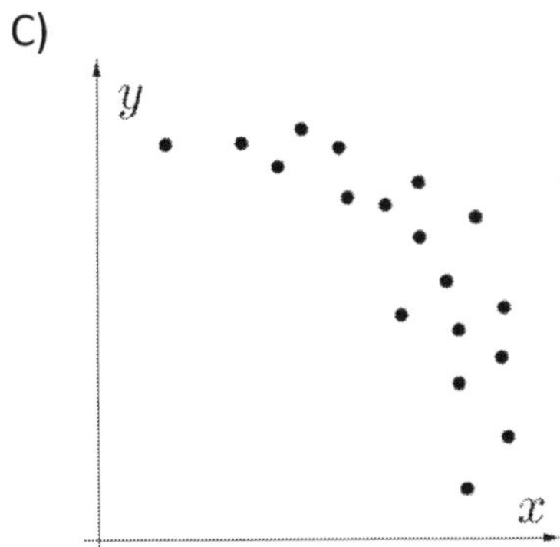

D)

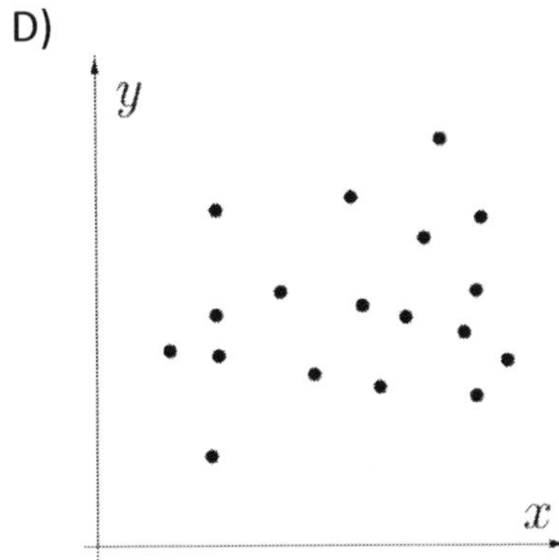

26.

$$1\ yard = 3\ feet$$
$$1\ foot = 12\ inches$$

George wants to tile the kitchen floor. The length of the kitchen is 3 yards, and the length of the tile is 4 inches. How many tiles are needed for one row?

A) 25
B) 26
C) 27
D) 28

27.

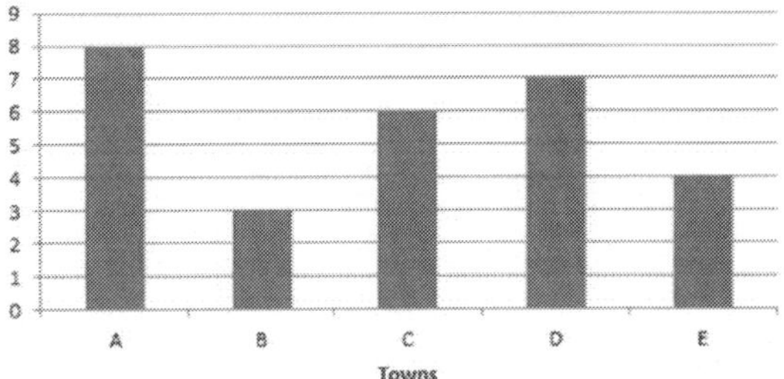

The number of citizens in 5 towns is shown in the graph above. If the minimum number of citizens in one of the 5 towns is 30,000, what is an appropriate label for the vertical axis of the graph?

A) Number of citizens (in hundreds)
B) Number of citizens (in thousands)
C) Number of citizens (in ten thousands)
D) Number of citizens (in hundred thousands)

28. If $|x| < 4$, what are the possible values for x?

A) $-4 < x < 4$
B) $-4 < x < 0$
C) $0 < x < 4$
D) $x < 4$

Questions 29 and 30 refer to the following information:

$$v = 40 + 4a$$

The velocity of an object depends on the acceleration a. The formula above shows the relationship between v, the speed of an object, in feet per second, and a, the acceleration, in feet per second squared.

29. Which of the following expresses the acceleration in terms of the velocity of an object?

A) $\frac{v-4}{40}$
B) $\frac{v-40}{4}$
C) $\frac{v+4}{40}$
D) $\frac{v+40}{4}$

30. At which of the following accelerations will the speed of an object be 50 feet per second?

A) 1.5
B) 2
C) 2.5
D) 3

31. Which of the following numbers is a solution of the inequality $3x - 5 > 6 - 2x$?

A) 0
B) 1
C) 2
D) 3

32.

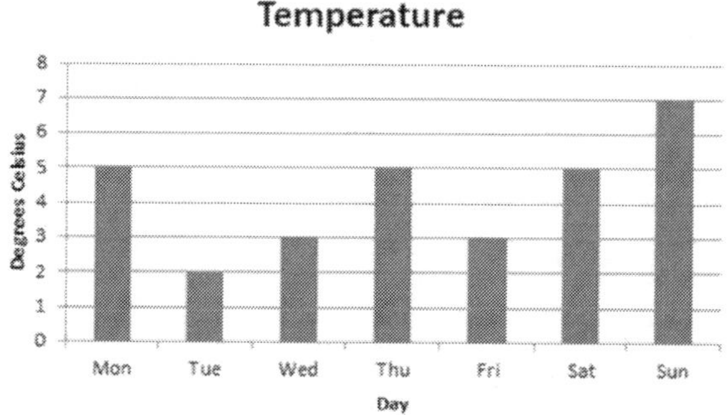

What is the mode of the data in the graph above?

A) 3
B) 4
C) 5
D) 6

33.

		Pets			
		Dogs	Cats	Parrots	Total
Gender	Female	12	18	12	42
	Male	24	6	8	38
	Total	36	24	20	80

The table above shows the number of pets according to their gender. What is the percent of female cats among all pets?

A) 20%
B) 22.5%
C) 25%
D) 27.5%

34.

The number of shirts sold in April						
21	45	12	16	32	25	12
7	13	25	21	8	14	7
9	12	21	16	7	26	8
25	11	5	16	12	27	5

What is the range of the data in the table above?

A) 5
B) 25

C) 40
D) 45

Questions 35 and 36 refer to the following information.

Level of gas in a tank

Liters of gas (l)
50
44
38
32
26
20
0 100 200 300 400 500
Kilometers (d)

The graph above displays the level of gas in the tank *l*, in liters, depending on the distance passed *d*, in kilometers.

35. What is the initial level of gas in the tank?

A) 0
B) 44
C) 50
D) 500

36. What is the level of gas in the tank after 300 kilometers passed?

A) 50
B) 44
C) 38
D) 32

37.

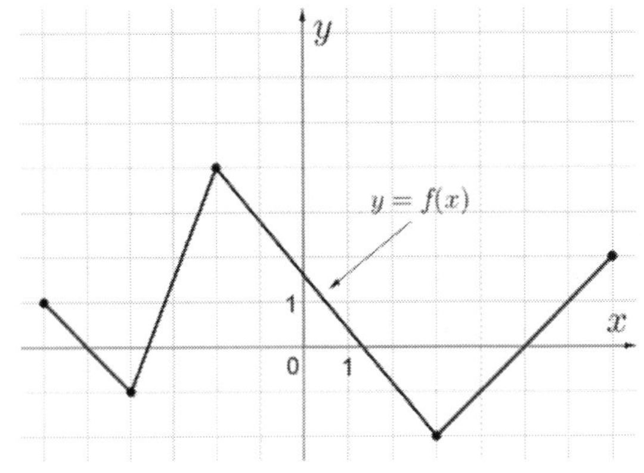

The complete graph of the function *f* is shown in the *xy*-plane above. What is the y-coordinate of the point which is the maximum of the function?

A) -4
B) -2
C) 2
D) 4

38.

$$y > x - 3$$
$$y < 4x + 3$$

Which of the following points is NOT the solution of the system of inequalities above?

A) (1,-1)
B) (2,3)
C) (-1,3)
D) (0,0)

39. There are 245 boys and girls in the cinema. If there are 23 girls more than boys, what is the number of girls?

A) 111
B) 114
C) 131
D) 134

40. Sarah lost 3 kg last week, and now she weighs 57 kg. What percentage of her mass did she lose?

A) 3%
B) 4.26%
C) 5%
D) 5.26%

41.

Years of experience of employees

	Less than 10	Between 10 and 20	Between 20 and 30	More than 30	Total
Males	12	14	8	6	40
Females	6	24	16	4	50
Total	18	38	24	10	90

The table above shows the number of employees based on their years of experience. If a person is chosen at random, what is the probability that she has less than 10 years of experience?

A) $\frac{1}{5}$
B) $\frac{1}{4}$
C) $\frac{1}{3}$
D) $\frac{1}{2}$

Questions 42 and 43 refer to the following information.

Number of students at Faculty of Natural Sciences and Mathematics

Department	Year			
	2010	2011	2012	2013
Math	120	90	110	86
Physics	86	90	96	108
Biology	94	76	88	92
Chemistry	108	120	115	103

The table above lists the number of students at the Faculty of Natural Sciences and Mathematics from 2010 to 2013.

42. Which year did the Math Department have the most students?

A) 2010
B) 2011
C) 2012
D) 2013

43. Which department had the least number of students?

A) Math
B) Physics
C) Biology
D) Chemistry

44.

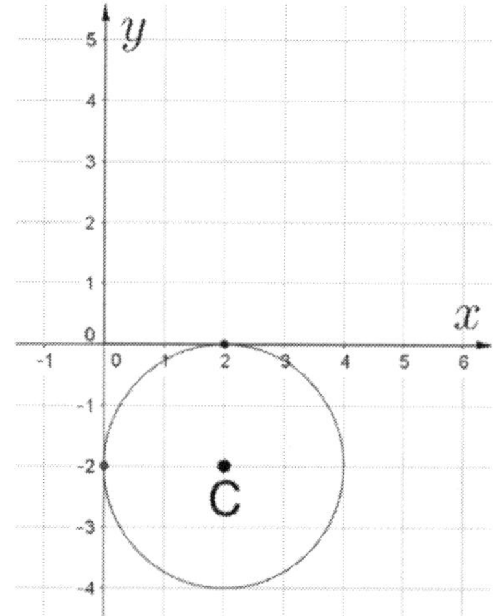

What is the equation of the circle in the graph above?

A) $(x-2)^2+(y+2)^2=4$
B) $(x+2)^2+(y-2)^2=4$
C) $(x-2)^2+(y+2)^2=2$
D) $(x+2)^2+(y-2)^2=2$

45.

$$P=\frac{1}{4}t^2+t-5$$

The profit P of a company, in millions of dollars, is given by the equation above where t is time in years. What is the profit of the company after 4 years?

A) \$1,000,000
B) \$2,000,000
C) \$3,000,000
D) \$4,000,000

46. There are 32 students in the class, and 12.5% of them are girls. How many boys are there in the class?

A) 20
B) 22
C) 24
D) 28

47. In the school restaurant, during the lunch break, Emma randomly chose 30 students and asked them if they like math. Eight of them answered positive. If the number of students in the school is 540, what is the expected number of students in the school who love math?

A) 64
B) 88
C) 144
D) 150

48.

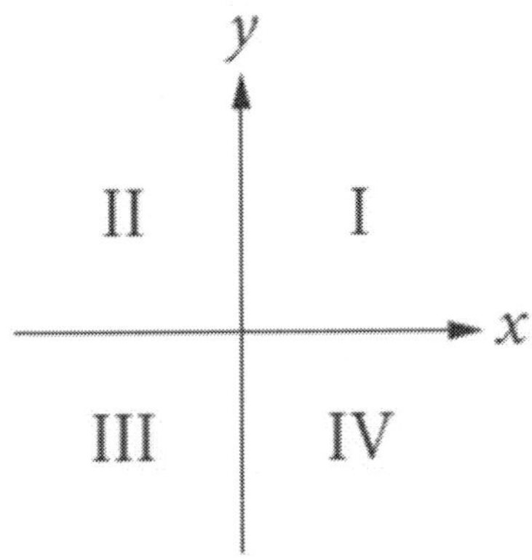

If a line $2x + 3y - 12 = 0$ is graphed in the xy-plane above, which quadrant contains no points of this line?

A) I
B) II
C) III
D) IV

49. For a polynomial $p(x)$, the value of $p(-1)$ is 0. Which of the following must be true about $p(x)$?

A) $p(1) - 1 = 0$
B) $p(-1) + 1 = 0$
C) $x - 1$ is a factor of $p(x)$
D) $x + 1$ is a factor of $p(x)$

50. The equation of parabola is $y = x^2 - 6x - 16$. Which of the following expressions is equivalent to this equation?

A) $y = (x + 8)(x - 2)$
B) $y = (x - 8)(x - 2)$
C) $y = (x - 8)(x + 2)$
D) $y = (x + 8)(x + 2)$

Student-Produced Responses

51. If $-5 < x < -3$ and $1 < y < 5$, what is one possible integer value for $x - y$?

52. Olivia weighs 68 kg. She loses 3 kg every month. After how many months will she weigh less than 55 kg?

53.

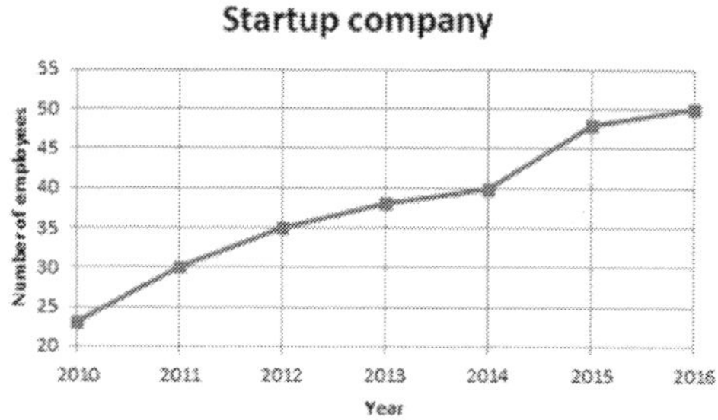

How many years was the number of employees in the company less than 40?

54. The speed of the train is $36\frac{km}{h}$. How many meters does the train pass in 1 second?

55.

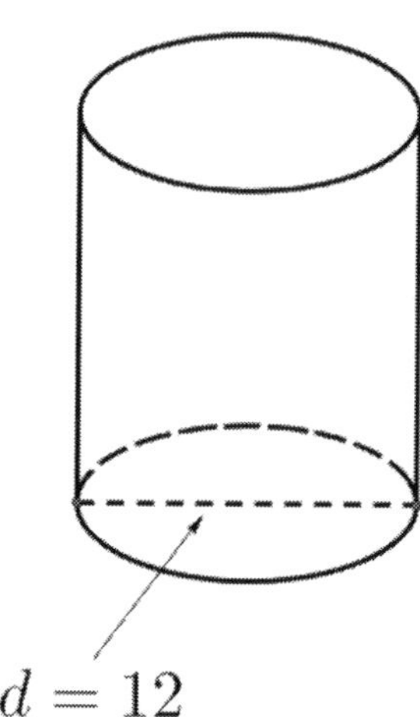

The gas tank is shown in the figure above. If its volume is 360π, what is its height?

56. For what value of x does function $y = \frac{x^2-6x+9}{x+4}$ intersect x-axis?

Questions 57 and 58 refer to the following information.

The number of employees in the company falls 6% each year. In 2010, there were 2,200 employees. The expression $2{,}200 \times (x)^t$ is used to estimate the number of employees after t years.

57. What is the value of x in the expression?

58. What is the number of employees after 5 years? (Round your answer to the nearest hundred)

No Test Material On This Page

Test 5 Answer Key

1	D	21	B	41	A
2	A	22	D	42	A
3	A	23	C	43	C
4	D	24	B	44	A
5	B	25	A	45	C
6	A	26	C	46	D
7	C	27	C	47	C
8	B	28	A	48	C
9	A	29	B	49	D
10	B	30	C	50	C
11	A	31	D	51	-9, -8, -7, -6, OR -5
12	C	32	C	52	5
13	A	33	B	53	4
14	D	34	C	54	10
15	C	35	C	55	10
16	-4	36	D	56	3
17	1.4	37	D	57	0.94
18	-2	38	C	58	1600
19	0.8 OR 4/5	39	D		
20	0	40	C		

TEST 6

ANSWER SHEET

Section 3

1 A B C D	4 A B C D	7 A B C D	10 A B C D	13 A B C D
2 A B C D	5 A B C D	8 A B C D	11 A B C D	14 A B C D
3 A B C D	6 A B C D	9 A B C D	12 A B C D	15 A B C D

16	17	18	19	20
/	/	/	/	/
.	.	.	.	.
0	0	0	0	0
1	1	1	1	1
2	2	2	2	2
3	3	3	3	3
4	4	4	4	4
5	5	5	5	5
6	6	6	6	6
7	7	7	7	7
8	8	8	8	8
9	9	9	9	9

Section 4

21 A B C D	27 A B C D	33 A B C D	39 A B C D	45 A B C D
22 A B C D	28 A B C D	34 A B C D	40 A B C D	46 A B C D
23 A B C D	29 A B C D	35 A B C D	41 A B C D	47 A B C D
24 A B C D	30 A B C D	36 A B C D	42 A B C D	48 A B C D
25 A B C D	31 A B C D	37 A B C D	43 A B C D	49 A B C D
26 A B C D	32 A B C D	38 A B C D	44 A B C D	50 A B C D

51

52

53

54

55

56

57

58

Section 3

Math Test – No Calculator
Allotted Time: 25 Minutes
Number of Questions: 20

Calculator **NOT** permitted.

Reference Formulas

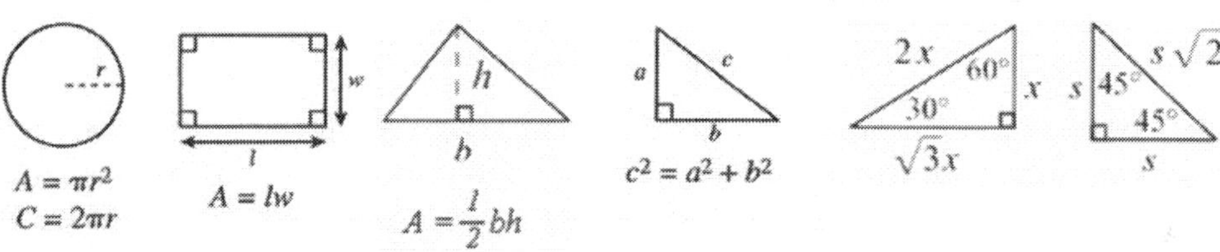

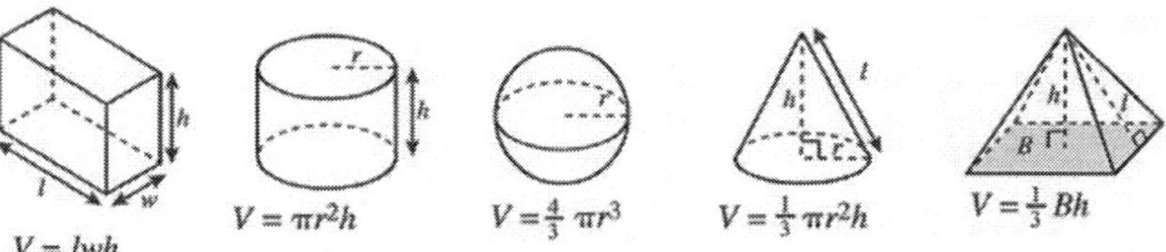

The number of degrees of arc in a circle is 360.
The number of radians of arc in a circle is 2π.
The sum of the measures in degrees of the angles of a triangle is 180.

1. What is the value of x that will satisfy both the equations $\frac{1}{x+y} = \frac{4}{27}$ and $\frac{1}{2-y} = \frac{4}{33}$?

   A. x=5
   B. x=1 ¾
   C. x=4
   D. x=3 ½

2. Identify each equation as a conditional equation, a contradiction equation or an identity equation.

   Equation 1: $4k - 5 = 2(2k - 3) + 1$
   Equation 2: $2(b - 4) = 2b - 7$
   Equation 3: $3x + 7 = 2x - 5$

   A. Equation 1 is a conditional equation; equations 2 and 3 are contradiction equations.
   B. Equation 1 and 2 are identity equations, equation 3 is a contradiction equation.
   C. Equation 1 is an identity equation, equation 2 is a conditional equation, and equation 3 is a contradiction equation.
   D. Equation 1 is an identity equation, equation 2 is a contradiction equation, and equation 3 is a conditional equation.

3. Thirty times the largest of the four consecutive integers is fifty-six more than seven times the sum of the four consecutive integers. What is the smallest integer?

   A. 6
   B. 7
   C. 8
   D. 9

4. A certain play sold a total of 300 tickets yesterday. The regular priced ticket cost $8 each and the discounted priced ticket cost $6 each. If the total revenue from ticket sales of the play was $2,040 yesterday, how many regular priced tickets were sold yesterday?

   A. 120 regular priced tickets sold
   B. 115 regular priced tickets sold
   C. 110 regular priced tickets sold
   D. 105 regular priced tickets sold

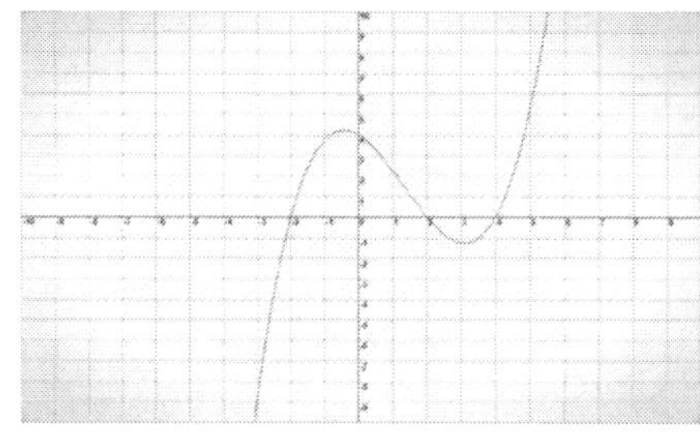

5. Find the sum of all the roots of the curve in the graph above.

   A. 4
   B. 3
   C. 2
   D. 1

A certain company manufactures two kinds of umbrella - ordinary and folding umbrellas. Each umbrella passes through two separate departments: assembly and sewing departments. The assembly department has only 200 labor hours available while the sewing department has 180 hours available. Other information regarding the products is presented below:

	Ordinary	Folding
Unit price of umbrella	\$20	\$30
Required hours (Assembly) to make 1 umbrella	2 hours	2 hours
Required hours (Sewing) to make 1 umbrella	2 hours	1 hour

6. What is the maximum possible profit the company can make from selling the two kinds of umbrellas?

   A. \$2,200.00
   B. \$1,800.00
   C. \$2,000.00
   D. \$2,300.00

7. Which of the following given statements below must be true?

   i. The largest possible factor to the polynomial equation $x^3 - 10x^2 + 33x - 36$ is 3.
   ii. The highest integral value of 'k' for which the quadratic equation $x^2 - 6x + k = 0$ have two real and distinct roots is 3.
   iii. $x^2 + bx + 72 = 0$ has two distinct integer roots; 10 values are only possible for 'b'.

   A. Only Statement i is true.
   B. Only Statement ii is true.
   C. Only Statement ii is true.
   D. All Statements are false.

8. The equation of a straight line is y=mx +c. If a straight line passes through the points (1, -2) and $(3\frac{1}{2}, 10\frac{1}{2})$, find the values of the slope and y-axis intercept of the straight line.

   A. Slope = 5 and y-axis intercept = 7
   B. Slope = -5 and y-axis intercept = −7
   C. Slope = 5 and y-axis intercept = −7
   D. Slope = 4 and y-axis intercept = −7

9. What is the difference of the highest value of x and the lowest value of y which simultaneously satisfy the equations $y = 5x - 4 - 2x^2$ and $y = 6x - 7$?

   A. 2
   B. 17
   C. -1/2
   D. 14 ½

10. Which of the following statements is correct?

    Statement 1: The value of x in $5x + 7 < 3(x + 1)$ is $x \leq 2$

    Statement 2: The value of x in $3(x - 2) + 4 > 2(2x - 3)$ is $x > 4$

    Statement 3: The value of x in $2x - 5 + 5 < 1$ is $x < 3$

    A. Statement 1
    B. Statement 2
    C. Statement 3
    D. All statements

11. What is the highest integral value of k for which the quadratic equation $x^2 - 6x + k = 0$ will have two real and distinct roots?

A. 8
B. 7
C. 6
D. 5

12. Which of the following is the graph of the equations $(x - 2)^2 + (y + 3)^2 = 4$ and $2x + 2y = -1$?

A.

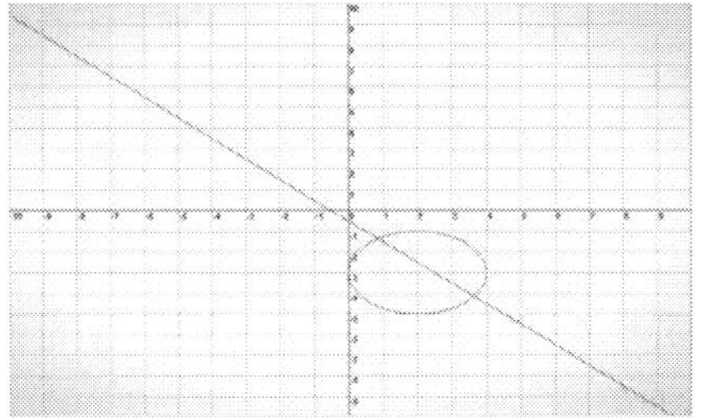

B.

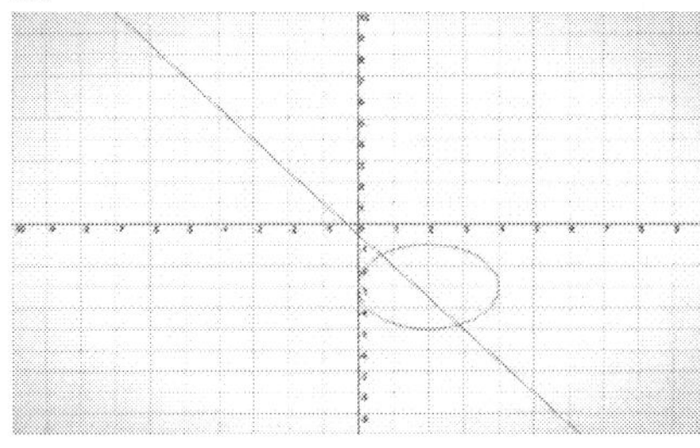

C.

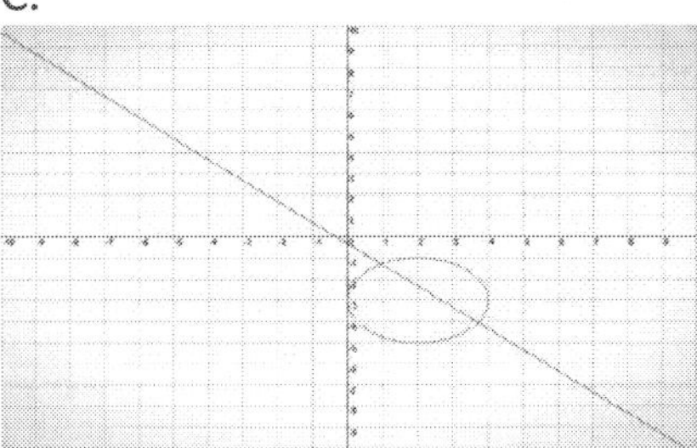

D.

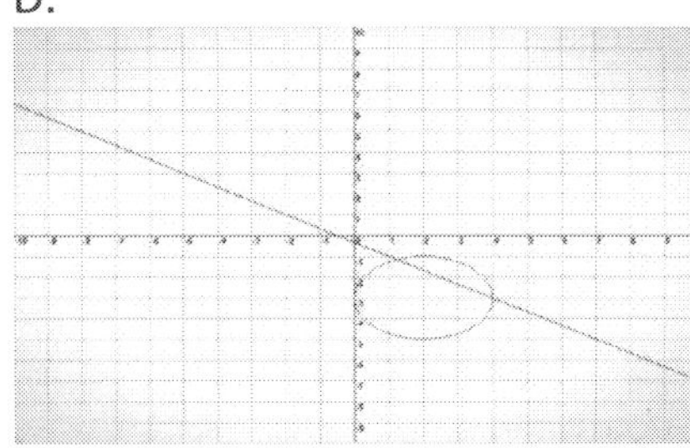

13. What is the equation of the quadratic equation having roots $\frac{1}{3}$ and −2.

A. $3x^2 + 5x - 2 = 0$
B. $3x^2 - 5x - 2 = 0$
C. $3x^2 + 5x + 2 = 0$

D. $-3x^2 + 5x - 2 = 0$

14. Ten times the reciprocal of a number is added to four. The result is equal to the quotient of twenty two and the number. Find the number.

A. 5
B. 4
C. 2
D. 3

15. Which of the following expressions is equivalent to $3 - \sqrt{8}$?

A. $\frac{1}{3-\sqrt{8}}$
B. $\frac{\sqrt{2}}{3-\sqrt{8}}$
C. $\frac{1}{3+\sqrt{8}}$
D. $\frac{\sqrt{2}}{3+\sqrt{8}}$

Student-Produced Responses

16. If $\sqrt{X+Y} = 6$ and $\sqrt{X} - \sqrt{Y} = 0$, then the value of X is?

17. What value of x will satisfy the equation $3x + 1 = \sqrt{3x^2 + 13}$?

The Poké Ball Factory, a facility located north of Laverre City in Kalos, has just started a competition for a 2D design of a poké ball for a newly discovered pokemon species.

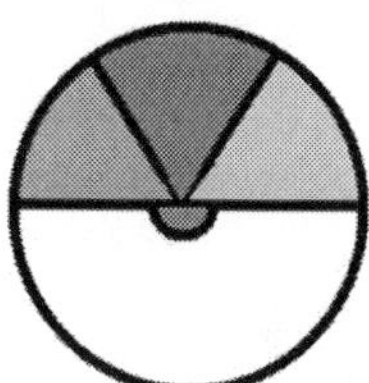

18. If the poké ball must be 5 cm in diameter and has to contain three colored sections of equal size, what is the area of each colored section? Express your answer to the nearest square centimeter.

19. An automobile manufacturer makes 4 models of scooters and each model comes with 5 options. How many different types of scooters does the manufacturer make?

20. Convert $\frac{\pi}{3}$ radians to degrees.

Section 4

Math Test – Calculator
Allotted Time: 55 Minutes
Number of Questions: 38

Calculator **IS** allowed.

Reference Formulas

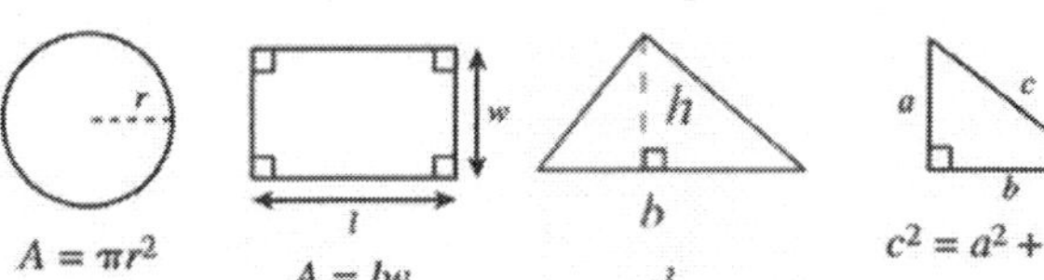

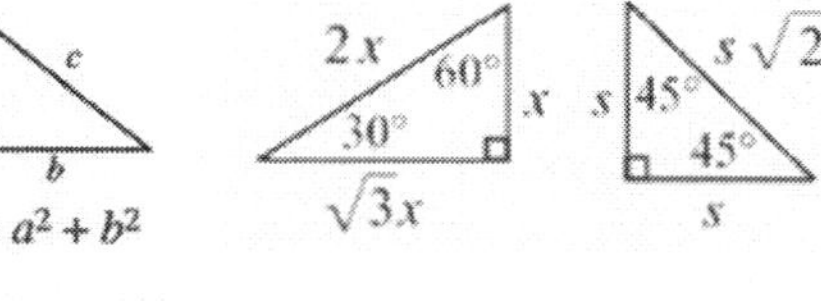

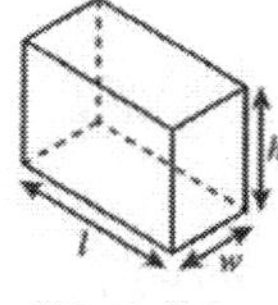

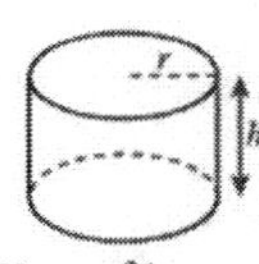

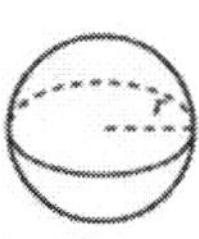

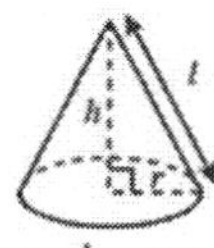

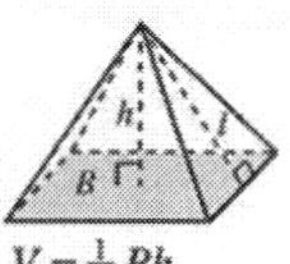

The number of degrees of arc in a circle is 360.
The number of radians of arc in a circle is 2π.
The sum of the measures in degrees of the angles of a triangle is 180.

21. In a certain cricket game last week, the Dolphins scored a total of 232 runs in the game. The score consisted of byes, wides and runs scored by the two best players in the team: George and Michael. The runs scored by the two players are 26 times the wides, and there are 8 more byes than wides. If the ratio of the runs scored by George to the runs scored by Michael was 6 to 7, how many runs was scored by George?

A. 88
B. 96
C. 102
D. 112

22. On the Starship Enterprise, Captain Picard continually asks the food replicator to brew him a cup of Earl Grey tea. The proper brewing temperature for Earl Grey tea is 210º F plus or minus 5 degrees. What could be the maximum and minimum brewing temperatures for Earl Grey tea?

A. Maximum Temperature = 205° and Minimum Temperature = 215°
B. Maximum Temperature = 200° and Minimum Temperature = 215°
C. Maximum Temperature = 205° and Minimum Temperature = 210°
D. Maximum Temperature = 200° and Minimum Temperature = 210°

23. Given that $x = 1$ and $\frac{x-y}{z} = 1$, which of the following is NOT a possible value for y?

A. -1
B. 0
C. 1
D. 2

24. What is the eighth decile group of the set of scores below?

14 22 17 21 30 28 37 7 23 32
24 17 20 22 27 19 26 21 15 29

A. Numbers 26 and 27
B. Numbers 27 and 28
C. Numbers 28 and 29
D. Numbers 30 and 31

25. In a certain batch of 100 microchips produced in a day, 73 are within the required tolerance standard, 17 are below the required standard, and the remainder are above the required tolerance standard. One microchip is randomly selected with replacement, and a second microchip is randomly selected, also with replacement. What is the probability that both microchips are within the required tolerance standard?

A. 57.29 %
B. 50.29 %
C. 59.29%
D. 53.29 %

26. A machine is producing lightbulbs in a certain factory on a daily basis. In a single day, 95% of the lightbulbs produced by the machine passes the quality control, and the remainder will not pass the quality control. If seven lightbulbs are selected at random, what is the probability that more than two of the seven lightbulbs will not pass quality control?

A. 0.18 %
B. 0.28 %
C. 0.38%
D. 0.48 %

27. How many different teams of eleven can be formed from a group of sixteen players?

A. 4,500
B. 4,368
C. 4,268
D. 4,400

28. A certain construction firm is building a mansion on top of Mount Crest Hill. The centerpiece of the mansion will be a huge stone block that the owner's name will be inscribed. The volume of the stone block must be 330 cubic yards. If the dimensions of the stone block is x yards high by (13x – 11) yards long and (13x – 15) yards wide, what is the height of the stone block?

A. 2 yards
B. 2.5 yards
C. 3 yards
D. 3.5 yards

29. What is the value of $5e^{0.5}$, correct to 5 significant figures?

A. 8.2446
B. 8.2436
C. 8.2456
D. 8.2466

30. Suppose P dollars in principal is invested in an account that earns interest annually. If after t years the investment grows to A dollars, then the annual rate of return, r, on the investment is given by $r = (\frac{A}{P})^{1/t} - 1$. Find the annual rate of return on \$8,000 that grew to \$11,220.41 after 5 years.

A. 4.5%
B. 5.0 %
C. 6.0 %
D. 7.%

31. A golfer hits a ball at an angle of 30°. The height of the ball y (in feet) can be represented by $y = -16x^2 + 60x$, where x is the time in seconds after the ball was hit. Find the maximum height of the ball and in how many seconds will the ball reach its maximum height?

A. The ball reaches maximum height of 25.25 feet after 1.875 sec.
B. The ball reaches maximum height of 26.25 feet after 1.575 sec.
C. The ball reaches maximum height of 27.25 feet after 1.775 sec.
D. The ball reaches maximum height of 26.25 feet after 1.875 sec.

32. A certain company spends x dollars in product development and y dollars in advertising. The company's profit is given to be $f(x, y) = 36{,}000 + 40x + 30y + \frac{xy}{100}$. If the company spends \$2,000 on product development and \$5,000 on advertising, how much was the company's profit?

A. \$ 388,000
B. \$ 377,000
C. \$ 366,000
D. \$ 355,000

33. The area of an ellipse is given as πab, where a is the length of semi-major axis and b is the length of the semi-minor axis. What is the area of a certain ellipse that has a major axis of 15 centimeters and minor axis of 9 centimeters?

A. 106.0 square centimeters
B. 105.0 square centimeters
C. 106.0 square centimeters
D. 106.5 square centimeters

34. A certain metal bolt consist of a cylinder head of diameter 1 centimeter and length of 2 millimeters, and a cylinder shaft of diameter 2 millimeters and length of 1.5 centimeters. What is the total volume of metal in 2,000 such bolts?

A. 408.4 cm^3
B. 408.5 cm^3
C. 408.6 cm^3
D. 408.7 cm^3

35. Jordan can run R miles in H hours, and then rides a bicycle B miles in three times the same number of hours. What was Jordan's average speed, in miles per hour, for these two activities combined?

A. $\frac{R+3B}{H}$

B. $\frac{4(R+B)}{H}$

C. $\frac{R+B}{4H}$

D. $\frac{R+B}{3H}$

36. Given that $(a-1)\times b = -b$, which of the following must be true?

A. $a = 1$ or $b = 0$
B. $a = 0$ or $b = 0$
C. $a = 0$ or $b = 1$
D. $a = 1$ or $b = 1$

37. Three years ago, Andrea's age was four times of Sally's age and four years from now, Andrea's age will be three times of Sally's age. Andrea is how many years older than Sally now?

A. 36
B. 42
C. 54
D. 60

38.

$$3x + 5y = \frac{1}{2}$$

$$2x - 3y = -1$$

In the system of linear equations above, if (x, y) is the solution to both equations, what is the value of $\frac{x}{y}$?

A. $-\frac{7}{8}$

B. $-\frac{7}{4}$

C. $\frac{7}{8}$

D. $\frac{7}{4}$

39. When graphed on the number line, which of the following inequalities has a solution set that is a single line segment of infinite length?

A. $|x| \leq 5$
B. $2 \leq 3x + 1 \leq 5$
C. $x \geq -2$
D. $0 \leq |2x+5| \leq 2$

40. In a certain quiz show, Cesar needs to get at least 80 points in order to advance to the next level. Each question answered correctly in the "True or False Section" is worth 3 points while each question answered correctly in the "Multiple Choice Section" is worth 2 points. Which of the following inequalities can represent the number of "True or False" questions m and the number of "Multiple Choice" questions n that Cesar needs to answer

correctly in order to advance to the next level?

A. $3m + 2n \geq 80$
B. $2m + 3n > 80$
C. $3m + 2n > 80$
D. $2m + 3n \geq 80$

41. The figure below shows the graph of line k on the xy-coordinate plane. Which of the following could be the slope of the line perpendicular to line k?

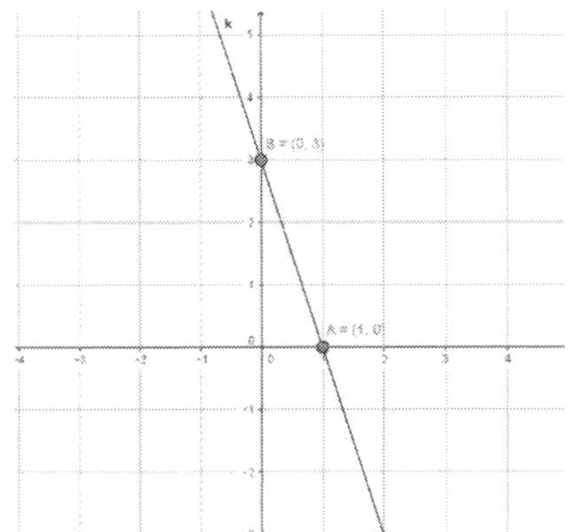

A. -3

B. $-\frac{1}{3}$

C. 3

D. $\frac{1}{3}$

42. The mean (arithmetic average) price of houses in a certain village is $1.5 million, and the standard deviation is $75,000. Find the price range for which at least 75% of the houses will sell.

A. At least 75% of all homes sold in the area will have a price range from $1,350,000 to $1,750,000
B. At least 75% of all homes sold in the area will have a price range from $1,650,000 to $2,350,000
C. At least 75% of all homes sold in the area will have a price range from $1,350,000 to $1,650,000
D. At least 75% of all homes sold in the area will have a price range from $1,850,000 to $2,350,000

43. You know that you will need $20,000 for your child's education in 18 years. If your account earns 4% compounded quarterly, how much would you need to deposit now to reach your goal?

A. $9,769.92
B. $9,669.92
C. $9,779.92
D. $9,760.92

44. What is the midrange of the twelve major earthquakes which has Richter magnitudes in the whole world for 2014 as reported by NASA. Magnitudes are shown below:

7.0 6.2 7.7 8.0 6.4 6.2
7.2 5.4 6.4 6.5 7.2 5.4

A. 1.2
B. 1.3
C. 1.8
D. 2.1

45. A certain track is 10 meters long. Each day, Jordan runs a total of 75 lengths of the track for exercise. How many kilometers did he run over a period of 15 days?

A. 11.50 km
B. 12.25 km
C. 11.25 km

D. 10.75km

46. If $R = \sqrt{25} + \sqrt[3]{25} + \sqrt[4]{25}$, then the value of R is?

A. Equal to 8
B. Between 8 and 9
C. Equal to 9
D. Greater than 9

47. Suppose P dollars in principal is invested in an account that earns interest annually. If after t years the investment grows to A dollars, then the annual rate of return, r, on the investment is given by r = $(\frac{A}{P})^{1/t}$ - 1. Find the annual rate of return on $8,000 that grew to $11,220.41 after 5 years.

A. 4.5%
B. 5.0 %
C. 6.0 %
D. 7.%

48. Find a fourth degree polynomial that is divisible by $x^2 - 4$ and is annulled by x = 3 and x = 5.

A. $y= x^4 - 8x^3 + 11x^2 +32x - 60$
B. $y= x^4 - 7x^3 + 11x^2 +32x - 60$
C. $y= x^4 - 8x^3 + 10x^2 +32x - 60$
D. $y= x^4 - 8x^3 + 11x^2 +30x - 60$

49. The roots of the polynomial $x^4 + 2x^3 - 9x^2 - 2x + 8 = 0$ are all integers. What is the difference between the biggest and the smallest root?

A. -6
B. -3
C. 1
D. 6

50. A certain patch of grass double in size every day. If it takes 48 days for the patch of grass to cover an entire field, how many days does it takes for the patch of grass to cover half of the field?

A. 24
B. 47
C. 48
D. 34

Student-Produced Responses

51. A piece of iron bar 273 feet long is cut into three pieces in the ratio of 3 to 7 to 11. What is the length of the longest piece?

52. If 3 workers can finish a certain job in 4 days, how many days will it take for 5 workers to complete the same job, if the rate of work remains constant?

53. A certain metal alloy consists of 60% copper, 25% zinc and 15% nickel. If a certain block of this metal alloy is 3.74 kilograms, what is the mass of nickel, in kilograms, in this block of metal alloy? Round your answer to two decimal places.

54. The sum of 7 terms of an arithmetic progression is 35 and the common difference is 1.2. What is the first term of the arithmetic progression?

55. Find the value of $(4 - 5i)(4 + 5i)$.

56. A certain map has a fractional scale of 1:24,000. If the length of a trail is 18.5 inches in the map, what is the actual distance, in miles, of the trail? (1 foot = 12 inches and 1 mile = 5,280 feet)

57. A certain bank gives a 5% interest on every deposit account every year. If you started with $50 in your deposit account, find the number of dollars in your account after 1 year?

58. A certain electric posts stands on a horizontal ground. If the angle of elevation of the top of the electric post is 23° at a distance 80 meters from the base of the electric post, what is the height of the electric post in meters?

No Test Material On This Page

Test 6 Answer Key

1	A	21	B	41	D
2	D	22	A	42	C
3	B	23	C	43	A
4	A	24	B	44	B
5	A	25	D	45	C
6	A	26	C	46	D
7	D	27	B	47	D
8	C	28	A	48	A
9	A	29	B	49	D
10	C	30	D	50	B
11	A	31	D	51	143
12	A	32	C	52	2.4
13	A	33	C	53	2.24
14	D	34	A	54	1.4
15	C	35	C	55	41
16	18	36	B	56	7
17	1 OR -2	37	B	57	52.5
18	3	38	A	58	34
19	20	39	B		
20	60	40	A		

FULL SOLUTIONS

TEST 1

1. The answer is C.

$$\frac{4x-k}{3}=-k \wedge k=-3$$
$$\frac{4x-(-3)}{3}=-(-3)$$
$$\frac{4x+3}{3}=3$$
$$3\times\frac{4x+3}{3}=3\times 3$$
$$4x+3=9$$
$$4x=9-3$$
$$4x=6$$
$$x=\frac{6}{4}=\frac{3}{2}$$

$$4x+3=4\times\frac{3}{2}+3=2\times 3+3=6+3=9$$

2. The answer is D.

$$\frac{6-2i}{2+5i}=\frac{6-2i}{2+5i}\times\frac{2-5i}{2-5i}=\frac{(6-2i)(2-5i)}{(2+5i)(2-5i)}=\frac{12-30i-4i+10i^2}{4-25i^2}=$$

$$=\frac{12-34i+10(-1)}{4-25(-1)}=\frac{12-34i-10}{4+25}=\frac{2-34i}{29}=\frac{2}{29}-\frac{34}{29}i$$

3. The answer is A.

The number of beds on one floor in the first hotel is $4n$. Since the hotel has m floors, the total number of beds in the first hotel is $4mn$. Similarly, the total number of beds in the second hotel is $3st$. Therefore, the total number of beds in both hotels is $4mn+3st$.

4. The answer is B.

H - altitude of the elevator above the ground
12 – the initial altitude of the elevator
t – unit of time
0.25 – the movement of the elevator in the unit of time t

5. The answer is D.

$$(7xy^2-3xy+6x)+(-5xy^2+2x+3xy)=$$
$$=7xy^2-3xy+6x-5xy^2+2x+3xy=2xy^2+8x=2x(y^2+4)$$

6. The answer is B.

C – the total cost of taxi
m – the number of miles passed
8 – the cost of start
4 – the increase in price after one mile passed

7. The answer is C.

$$v = \sqrt{\frac{GM}{r}}$$

$$v^2 = \left(\sqrt{\frac{GM}{r}}\right)^2$$

$$v^2 = \frac{GM}{r}$$

$$v^2 r = GM$$

$$r = \frac{GM}{v^2}$$

8. The answer is A.

$$\frac{a}{3b} = -6$$
$$a = -6 \times 3b$$
$$a = -18b$$

$$\frac{a}{2} + 9b = -\frac{18b}{2} + 9b = -9b + 9b = 0$$

9. The answer is C.

$$\frac{x}{2} - (y + 1) = x$$
$$x - \frac{y}{3} = 5$$

$$\frac{x}{2} - y - 1 - x = 0$$
$$3x - 3 \times \frac{y}{3} = 3 \times 5$$

$$2 \times \frac{x}{2} - 2y - 2 \times 1 - 2x = 2 \times 0$$
$$3x - y = 15$$

$$x - 2y - 2 - 2x = 0$$
$$3x - y = 15$$

$$-x - 2y = 2$$
$$3x - y = 15$$

$$-3x - 6y = 6$$
$$3x - y = 15$$
$$-7y = 21$$
$$y = -\frac{21}{7} = -3$$

$$3x - y = 15$$
$$3x - (-3) = 15$$
$$3x + 3 = 15$$
$$3x = 12$$
$$x = \frac{12}{3} = 4$$

10. The answer is C.

$$f(5) = 3 \Leftrightarrow 3 = \sqrt{5^2 - 2a} \Leftrightarrow 3^2 = \left(\sqrt{5^2 - 2a}\right)^2 \Leftrightarrow 9 = 25 - 2a \Leftrightarrow$$
$$\Leftrightarrow 9 - 25 = -2a \Leftrightarrow 2a = 16 \Leftrightarrow a = 8$$
$$f(-5) = \sqrt{(-5)^2 - 2 \times 8} = \sqrt{25 - 16} = \sqrt{9} = 3$$

11. The answer is B.

$$m = n$$
$$7 + 0.5h = 9 + 0.25h$$
$$0.5h - 0.25h = 9 - 7$$
$$0.25h = 2$$
$$h = \frac{2}{0.25} = \frac{200}{25} = 8$$

$m = 7 + 0.5h = 7 + 0.5 \times 8 = 7 + 4 = 11$

12. The answer is A.

Find equation of line which passes through the points (-4,-2) and (1,-8).

$x_1 = -4, y_1 = -2, x_2 = 1, y_2 = -8$

$y - y_1 = \frac{y_2 - y_1}{x_2 - x_1}(x - x_1)$

$y - (-2) = \frac{-8 - (-2)}{1 - (-4)}\left(x - (-4)\right)$

$y + 2 = \frac{-8 + 2}{1 + 4}(x + 4)$

$y + 2 = -\frac{6}{5}(x + 4)$

$y + 2 = -\frac{6}{5}x - \frac{24}{5}$

$5y + 5 \times 2 = -5 \times \frac{6}{5}x - 5 \times \frac{24}{5}$

$5y + 10 = -6x - 24$

$6x + 5y + 10 + 24 = 0$

$6x + 5y + 34 = 0$

Now substitute coordinates of points in the equation of line to check whether they lie on a line.

$x = -9, y = 4$

$6(-9) + 5 \times 4 + 34 = 0$

$-54 + 20 + 34 = 0$

$-34 + 34 = 0$

$0 = 0$

Therefore, point (-9,4) lies on a line which passes through the points (-4,-2) and (1,-8).

13. The answer is B.

$\frac{1}{\frac{1}{x-1} - \frac{1}{x+1}} = \frac{1}{\frac{1(x+1)}{(x-1)(x+1)} - \frac{1(x-1)}{(x-1)(x+1)}} = \frac{1}{\frac{x+1-(x-1)}{(x-1)(x+1)}} =$

$= \frac{(x-1)(x+1)}{x+1-x+1} = \frac{x^2-1}{2}$

14. The answer is B.

$\frac{4^x 8^y}{2^z} = \frac{(2^2)^x (2^3)^y}{2^z} = \frac{2^{2x} 2^{3y}}{2^z} = 2^{2x+3y-z} = 2^{10} = 2^{2\times 5} = (2^2)^5 = 4^5$

15. The answer is B.

$$(ax-2)(bx-5)=cx^2-19x+d$$
$$abx^2-5ax-2bx+10=cx^2-19x+d$$
$$abx^2-(5a+2b)x+10=cx^2-19x+d$$

$$d=10$$

$$a+b=5 \Longrightarrow a=5-b$$
$$5a+2b=19$$
$$5(5-b)+2b-19=0$$
$$25-5b+2b-19=0$$
$$6-3b=0$$
$$6=3b$$
$$b=2$$
$$a=5-b=5-2=3$$

$$ab=c$$
$$3\times 2=c$$
$$6=c$$

$$\sqrt{\frac{cd}{15}}=\sqrt{\frac{6\times 10}{15}}=\sqrt{4}=2$$

16. The answer is: -3

$$x^4-81=0$$
$$(x^2)^2-9^2=0$$
$$(x^2-9)(x^2+9)=0$$
$$(x^2-3^2)(x^2+9)=0$$
$$(x-3)(x+3)(x^2+9)=0$$
$$x-3=0 \Longrightarrow x=3$$
$$x+3=0 \Longrightarrow x=-3$$
$x^2+9=0 \Longrightarrow x^2=-9 \Longrightarrow x=\pm\sqrt{-9} \Longrightarrow$ no solution

$$x<0 \Longrightarrow x=-3$$

17. The answer is: 24

The stick and its shadow form a right triangle, similar to the triangle formed by the tree and its shadow. This is because we assume that sunrays are parallel and the ground is flat. Corresponding sides of similar triangles are proportional. In this case the quotient of heights of the tree and stick is equal to the quotient of the lengths of their shadows.

$$\frac{\{The\ height\ of\ the\ tree\}}{\{The\ height\ of\ the\ stick\}} = \frac{\{The\ length\ of\ the\ shadow\ of\ the\ tree\}}{\{The\ length\ of\ the\ shadow\ of\ the\ stick\}}$$

$$\frac{x}{3} = \frac{12}{1.5}$$

$$1.5x = 3 \times 12$$

$$x = \frac{36}{1.5} = \frac{360}{15} = \frac{120}{5} = 24$$

18. The answer is: 2

$$\frac{x-2}{3} + \frac{y}{2} = 1 + \frac{x}{4}$$
$$2x - 5y = -11$$

$$12 \times \frac{x-2}{3} + 12 \times \frac{y}{2} = 12 \times 1 + 12 \times \frac{x}{4}$$
$$2x - 5y = -11$$

$$4(x-2) + 6y = 12 + 3x$$
$$2x - 5y = -11$$

$$4x - 8 + 6y - 12 - 3x = 0$$
$$2x - 5y = -11$$

$$x + 6y = 20$$
$$2x - 5y = -11$$

$$5x + 30y = 100$$
$$12x - 30y = -66$$

$$5x + 30y + 12x - 30y = 100 - 66$$
$$17x = 34$$
$$x = 2$$

19. The answer is: $\frac{15}{17}$

$$\tan x = \frac{\sin x}{\cos x} = \frac{15}{8} \Longrightarrow 8\sin x = 15\cos x \Longrightarrow \cos x = \frac{8}{15}\sin x$$

$$\sin^2 x + \cos^2 x = 1$$

$$\sin^2 x + \left(\frac{8}{15}\sin x\right)^2 = 1$$
$$\sin^2 x + \frac{64}{225}\sin^2 x = 1$$
$$225\sin^2 x + 225 \times \frac{64}{225}\sin^2 x = 225 \times 1$$
$$225\sin^2 x + 64\sin^2 x = 225$$
$$289\sin^2 x = 225$$
$$\sin^2 x = \frac{225}{289}$$
$$\sin x = \sqrt{\frac{225}{289}} = \frac{15}{17}$$

20. The answer is: 2

$$x = \sqrt{4 - 2\sqrt{3}} + \sqrt{4 + 2\sqrt{3}}$$

$$x^2 = \left(\sqrt{4 - 2\sqrt{3}} + \sqrt{4 + 2\sqrt{3}}\right)^2$$

$$x^2 = \left(\sqrt{4 - 2\sqrt{3}}\right)^2 + 2\sqrt{4 - 2\sqrt{3}}\sqrt{4 + 2\sqrt{3}} + \left(\sqrt{4 + 2\sqrt{3}}\right)^2$$

$$x^2 = 4 - 2\sqrt{3} + 2\sqrt{(4 - 2\sqrt{3})(4 - 2\sqrt{3})} + 4 + 2\sqrt{3}$$

$$x^2 = 8 + 2\sqrt{4^2 - (2\sqrt{3})^2}$$

$$x^2 = 8 + 2\sqrt{16 - 12}$$

$$x^2 = 8 + 2 \times \sqrt{4}$$

$$x^2 = 8 + 2 \times 2$$

$$x^2 = 12$$

$$x = \sqrt{12} = \sqrt{4 \times 3} = 2\sqrt{3}$$

$$\frac{\sqrt{4 - 2\sqrt{3}} + \sqrt{4 + 2\sqrt{3}}}{\sqrt{3}} = \frac{2\sqrt{3}}{\sqrt{3}} = 2$$

21. The answer is C.

Minute	8	9	10	11	12
Speed	40	30	20	30	40

$$\{Average\ Speed\} = \frac{40+30+20+30+40}{5} = \frac{160}{5} = 32$$

22. The answer is D.

Parallel lines have equal slopes. Find the slope of a line $x - 2y = -4$.

$x - 2y = -4$
$-2y = -x - 4$
$2y = x + 4$
$y = \frac{1}{2}x + 2$
$k = \frac{1}{2}$

The coordinates of x-intercept are (x,0).

$y = kx - \frac{5}{2}$
$0 = \frac{1}{2}x - \frac{5}{2}$
$-\frac{1}{2}x = -\frac{5}{2}$
$x = 5$

23. The answer is D.

$\alpha + 2\alpha + 3\alpha = 180^o$
$6\alpha = 180^o$
$\alpha = 30^o$
$\sphericalangle BAE = \sphericalangle CDE \Longrightarrow x^o = 2\alpha = 2 \times 30^o = 60^o$

24. The answer is A.

$x^2 - 6x + 9 + 4 = 5$
$(x-3)^2 + 4 = 5$
$(x-3)^2 = 5 - 4$
$(x-3)^2 = 1$
$x - 3 = \pm\sqrt{1}$
$x - 3 = \pm 1$
$x = 3 \pm 1$
$x = 3 + 1 = 4 \vee x = 3 - 1 = 2$

$x < 4 \Longrightarrow x = 2$

$x^2 + 3 = 2^2 + 3 = 4 + 3 = 7$

25. The answer is D.

A graph with no association between *x* and *y* would have the points on the graph spread out. Of the four graphs, the points on the graph D are the most spread out.

26. The answer is C.

$$1\ km = 1{,}000\ m \Longrightarrow 1\ m = \frac{1}{1{,}000}\ km$$
$$1\ hour = 60\ minutes = (60 \times 60)\ seconds = 3{,}600\ seconds$$
$$1\ second = \frac{1}{3{,}600}\ hours$$

$$v = \frac{s}{t} = \frac{100\ m}{9.58\ s} = \frac{\frac{100}{1{,}000}km}{\frac{9.58}{3{,}600}h} = \frac{100 \times 3{,}600}{1{,}000 \times 9.58}\frac{km}{h} = \frac{360{,}000}{9{,}580}\frac{km}{h} \approx 37.58\frac{km}{h}$$

27. The answer is C.

The average number of citizens in 5 towns on the graph is $\frac{8+3+6+7+4}{5} = 5.6$
$$\frac{56{,}000}{5.6} = \frac{560{,}000}{56} = 10{,}000$$
Therefore, an appropriate label for the vertical axis of the graph is ten thousands.

28. The answer is A.

$$|3 - x| < 2$$
$$-2 < 3 - x < 2$$
$$-3 - 2 < -3 + 3 - x < -3 + 2$$
$$-5 < -x < -1$$
$$-5(-1) < -x(-1) < -1(-1)$$
$$5 > x > 1$$
$$1 < x < 5$$

29. The answer is B.

$$u = \frac{v + u'}{1 + \frac{vu'}{c^2}}$$

$$u=\frac{v+u'}{\frac{c^2}{c^2}+\frac{vu'}{c^2}}=\frac{v+u'}{\frac{c^2+vu'}{c^2}}=\frac{\frac{v+u'}{1}}{\frac{c^2+vu'}{c^2}}=\frac{c^2(v+u')}{c^2+vu'}=\frac{c^2v+c^2u'}{c^2+vu'}$$

$$u(c^2+vu')=c^2v+c^2u'$$

$$uc^2+uvu'=c^2v+c^2u'$$

$$uvu'-c^2u'=c^2v-uc^2$$

$$u'(uv-c^2)=c^2(v-u)$$

$$u'=\frac{c^2(v-u)}{uv-c^2}=\frac{v-u}{\frac{uv-c^2}{c^2}}=\frac{v-u}{\frac{uv}{c^2}-1}=\frac{u-v}{1-\frac{uv}{c^2}}$$

30. The answer is D.

$$v=100{,}000, u=110{,}000, c=300{,}000$$

$$u=\frac{v+u'}{1+\frac{vu'}{c^2}}$$

$$110{,}000=\frac{100{,}000+u'}{1+\frac{100{,}000u'}{300{,}000^2}}$$

$$110{,}000\left(1+\frac{100{,}000u'}{300{,}000^2}\right)=100{,}000+u'$$

$$110{,}000+110{,}000\times\frac{100{,}000u'}{300{,}000^2}=100{,}000+u'$$

$$10{,}000+0.12u'=u'$$

$$10{,}000=u'-0.12u'$$

$$10{,}000=0.88u'$$

$$u'=\frac{10{,}000}{0.88}=11{,}363.64$$

31. The answer is A.

$$\frac{x-2}{3}-x\geq 1-\frac{x+1}{6}$$

$$6\times\frac{x-2}{3}-6x\geq 6\times 1-6\times\frac{x+1}{6}$$

$2(x-2)-6x \geq 6-1(x+1)$

$2x-4-6x \geq 6-x-1$

$-4x-4 \geq 5-x$

$-4x+x \geq 5+4$

$-3x \geq 9$

$3x \leq -9$

$x \leq -\frac{9}{3}$

$x \leq -3$

32. The answer is C.

The following numbers appear in the graph: 5, 2, 3, 5, 4, 5, 7.

$$mean = \frac{5+2+3+5+4+5+7}{7} = \frac{31}{7} \approx 4.43$$

The temperature on Friday was 4°C. Therefore, on Friday the temperature was the closest to the average weekly temperature.

33. The answer is D.

$$\frac{\{Number\ of\ female\ dogs\ and\ parrots\}}{\{Total\ number\ of\ female\ pets\}} \times 100\% = \frac{12+12}{42} \times 100\% \approx 57\%$$

34. The answer is A.

For all 4 rows:

$$mean = \frac{\{sum\ of\ all\ values\}}{\{number\ of\ values\}} = \frac{448}{28} = 16$$

When you ommit last row:

$$mean = \frac{\{sum\ of\ all\ values\}}{\{number\ of\ values\}} = \frac{357}{21} = 17$$

$$difference = 17 - 16 = 1$$

35. The answer is A.

When the car passes 100 kilometers, the level of gas drops from 50 liters to 44 liters. So, the car needs 6 liters of gas to pass 100 kilometers, and 3 liters to pass 50 kilometers. In order to pass 650 kilometers, car needs $6 \times 6 + 3 = 39$ liters. So, the level og gas in the tank after 650 kilometers passed is $50 - 39 = 11$ liters.

36. The answer is B.

When the car passes 100 kilometers, the level of gas drops from 50 liters to 44 liters. So, the car needs 6 liters of gas to pass 100 kilometers.

$$\frac{100\,km}{6\,l} = 16.67\frac{km}{l}$$

37. The answer is A.

When the values of x increases and corresponding values of y increases, the function increases. So, the function increases when the line is moving up. According to graph, the function increases for $-4 < x < -2 \wedge 3 < x < 7$.

38. The answer is B.

If (0,0) is a solution then we have:

$(0,0) \Rightarrow x = 0, y = 0 \Rightarrow ax + by < a \Rightarrow a0 + b0 < a \Rightarrow 0 < a$

So, if a is positive, point (0,0) is a solution. Therefore, $a \leq 0$.

39. The answer is A.

x – mother's age
y – son's age

Mother is 18 years older than her son: $x - y = 18$
Three years ago, she was 3 times older than her son: $x - 3 = 3(y - 3)$

$x - y = 18$
$x - 3 = 3(y - 3)$

$x = y + 18$
$y + 18 - 3 = 3y - 9$
$15 + 9 = 3y - y$
$24 = 2y$
$y = \frac{24}{2} = 12$
$x = y + 18 = 12 + 18 = 30$

$x + y = 30 + 12 = 42$

40. The answer is C.

x – the initial price
y – final price
$y = x \times 1.12 \times 0.88$
$y = 0.9856x$
$y = 0.9856x \times 100\% = 98.56\%x$
The final price is 98.56% of the initial price. Therefore, the initial price changed for $100\% - 98.56 = 1.44\%$

41. The answer is C.

Years of experience of employees

	Less than 10	Between 10 and 20	Between 20 and 30	More than 30	Total
Males	12	14	8	6	40
Females	6	24	16	4	50
Total	18	38	24	10	90

There are $14 + 8 = 22$ employees with more than 10 and less than 30 years of experience.
Total number of employees with less than 30 years of experience is $18 + 38 + 24 = 80$.
$\frac{22}{80} = \frac{11}{40}$

42. The answer is C.

Number of students at Faculty of Natural Sciences and Mathematics

Department	Year			
	2010	2011	2012	2013
Math	120	90	110	86
Physics	86	90	96	108
Biology	94	76	88	92
Chemistry	108	120	115	103

$$\frac{108 - 90}{2013 - 2011} = \frac{18}{2} = 9$$

43. The answer is A.

Math Department: $\frac{120+90+110+86}{4} = \frac{406}{4} = 101.5$
Physics Department: $\frac{86+90+96+108}{4} = \frac{380}{4} = 95$

Biology Department: $\frac{94+76+88+92}{4} = \frac{350}{4} = 87.5$
Chemistry Department: $\frac{108+120+115+103}{4} = \frac{446}{4} = 111.5$

All departments:
$$\frac{101.5 + 95 + 87.5 + 111.5}{4} = \frac{395.5}{4} = 98.875$$

Department	Biology	Physics	All	Math	Chemistry
Average	87.5	95	98.875	101.5	111.5

Physics: $98.875 - 95 = 3.875$
Math: $101.5 - 98.875 = 2.625$
Therefore, the Math Department has the average of students closest to the average number of all students at the Faculty of Natural Sciences and Mathematics from 2010 to 2013.

44. The answer is B.

$$x^2 + y^2 - 4x + 8y - 5 = 0$$
$$x^2 - 4x + y^2 + 8y - 5 = 0$$
$$x^2 - 4x + 4 - 4 + y^2 + 8y + 16 - 16 - 5 = 0$$
$$x^2 - 4x + 4 + y^2 + 8y + 16 = 4 + 16 + 5$$
$$(x-2)^2 + (y+4)^2 = 25$$

The equation of the circle is $(x-p)^2 + (y-q)^2 = r^2$, where the center of the circle is $C(p,q)$ and radius is r.

$$r^2 = 25 \Longrightarrow r = \sqrt{25} = 5$$

45. The answer is C.

$$\frac{1}{4}t^2 + t - 5 > 0$$
$$4 \times \frac{1}{4}t^2 + 4t - 4 \times 5 > 0$$
$$t^2 + 4t - 20 > 0$$
$$t^2 + 4t - 20 = 0$$
$$a = 1, b = 4, c = -20$$
$$t_{1,2} = \frac{-b \pm \sqrt{b^2 - 4ac}}{2a} = \frac{-4 \pm \sqrt{4^2 - 4 \times 1 \times (-20)}}{2 \times 1} = \frac{-4 \pm \sqrt{16 + 80}}{2} =$$
$$= \frac{-4 \pm \sqrt{96}}{2} = \frac{-4 \pm \sqrt{16 \times 6}}{2} = \frac{-4 \pm 4\sqrt{6}}{2} = -2 \pm 2\sqrt{6} = \pm 2(\sqrt{6} - 1)$$

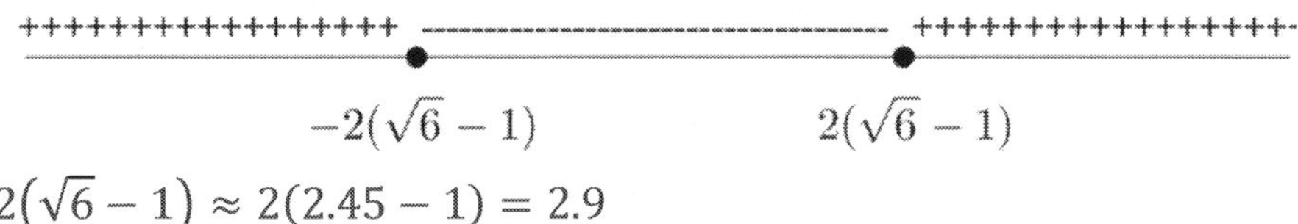

$2(\sqrt{6}-1) \approx 2(2.45-1) = 2.9$

Therefore, the company started making profit after 3rd year.

46. The answer is D.

S – Sarah's height
N – Noah's height
J – Johua's height

$$N = S + 25\%S = 160 + \frac{25}{100} \times 160 = 160 + 40 = 200$$

$$J = N + 5\%N = 200 + \frac{5}{100} \times 200 = 200 + 10 = 210$$

47. The answer is B.

$$\frac{\{Visitors\ on\ a\ photo\ with\ green\ hats\}}{\{All\ visitors\ on\ a\ photo\}} = \frac{\{All\ visitors\ with\ green\ hats\}}{\{All\ visitors\}}$$

$2{:}\,120 = 300{:}\,x$

$2x = 300 \times 120$

$$x = \frac{300 \times 120}{2} = 300 \times 60 = 18{,}000$$

48. The answer is A.

Solve the system of inequalities $11 - 3y < 4x$ and $4x - y > 7$ graphically.

$11 - 3y < 4x$

x	2	-1
y	1	5

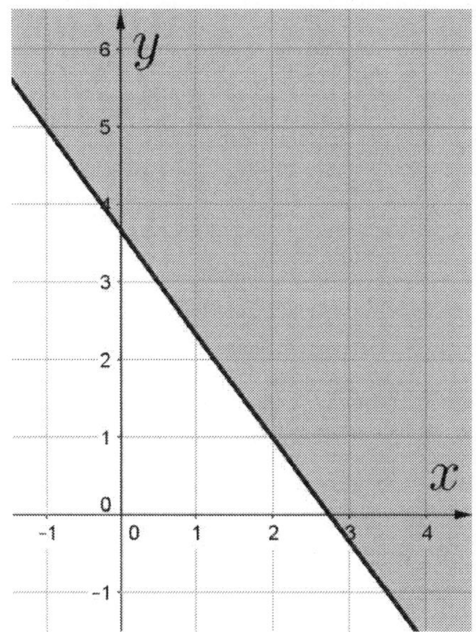

$4x - y > 7$

x	2	3
y	1	5

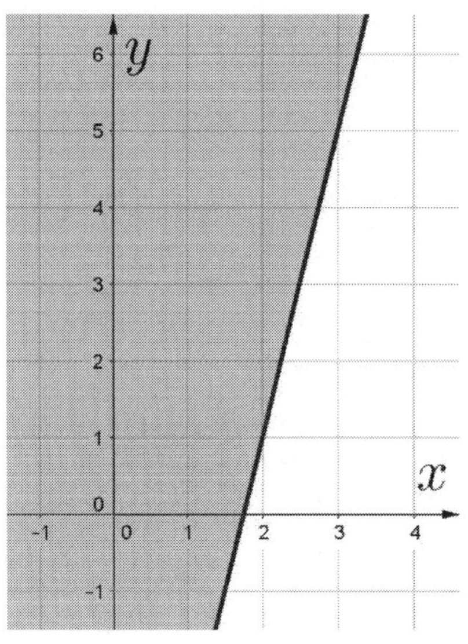

$11 - 3y < 4x$ and $4x - y > 7$

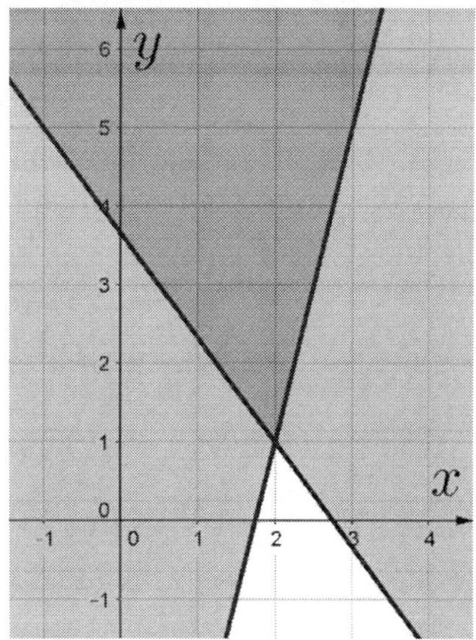

Therefore, quadrants I and II contain solutions to the system of inequalities.

49. The answer is A.

$x = 0$
$p(x) + p(-x) = 0$
$p(0) + p(-0) = 0$
$p(0) + p(0) = 0$
$2p(0) = 0 \Longrightarrow p(0) = 0 \div 2 \Longrightarrow p(0) = 0$

50. The answer is B.

The equation of parabola is $y = a(x - x_1)(x - x_2)$, where x_1 and x_2 are x-intercepts.
$x_1 = -1, x_2 = 4$

$y = a(x - x_1)(x - x_2)$
$y = a\big(x - (-1)\big)(x - 4)$
$y = a(x + 1)(x - 4)$

Y-intercept is at -1, which means that parabola passes through the point (0,-1).
$(0, -1) \Longrightarrow x = 0, y = -1$
$y = a(x + 1)(x - 4)$
$-1 = a(0 + 1)(0 - 4)$
$-1 = a \times 1 \times (-4)$
$-1 = -4a$
$a = \frac{1}{4}$

The equation of parabola is $y = \frac{1}{4}(x+1)(x-4)$

The x-coordinate of vertex is the midpoint of segment which endpoints are x-intercepts of parabola.

$$x = \frac{-1+4}{2} = \frac{3}{2}$$

Find y-coordinate of a vertex by substituting x in the equation of parabola.

$$y = \frac{1}{4}(x+1)(x-4) = \frac{1}{4}\left(\frac{3}{2}+1\right)\left(\frac{3}{2}-4\right) = \frac{1}{4}\left(\frac{3}{2}+\frac{2}{2}\right)\left(\frac{3}{2}-\frac{8}{2}\right) = \frac{1}{4}\times\frac{5}{2}\left(-\frac{5}{2}\right)$$

$$y = -\frac{25}{16}$$

Therefore, the coordinates of a vertex are $\left(\frac{3}{2}, -\frac{25}{16}\right)$

51. The answer is: 1 or 2

$$\left|\frac{2-5x}{3}\right| < 4$$

$$-4 < \frac{2-5x}{3} < 4$$

$$3 \times (-4) < 3 \times \frac{2-5x}{3} < 3 \times 4$$

$$-12 < 2-5x < 12$$

$$-2-12 < -2+2-5x < -2+12$$

$$-14 < -5x < 10$$

$$14 > 5x > -10$$

$$-10 < 5x < 14$$

$$-\frac{10}{5} < \frac{5x}{5} < \frac{14}{5}$$

$$-5 < x < 2.8$$

Therefore, possible values for x are 1 or 2.

52. The answer is: 14

x – number of T-shirts

$$240 + 2 \times 42 + 12x \le 500$$

$$12x \le 500 - 240 - 84$$

$$12x \le 176$$

$$x \le \frac{176}{12}$$

$$x \le \frac{44}{3}$$

$$x \leq 14\frac{2}{3}$$

Therefore, Sophia can buy at most 14 T-shirts.

53. The answer is: 4

The number of employees in 2011: 30.
The number of employees in 2016: 50.

$$\frac{\{Employees\ in\ 2016\} - \{Employees\ in\ 2011\}}{2016 - 2011} = \frac{50 - 30}{5} = \frac{20}{5} = 4$$

54. The answer is: 5

$$v = \frac{s}{t}$$

$v_1 = \frac{s_1}{t_1}$ – Joshua's speed

$v_2 = \frac{s_2}{t_2}$ – Joshua's speed

Time of traveling until they meet each other is equal for both of them: $t_1 = t_2 = t$.
The sum of distances they pass is equal to the distance from A to B: $s_1 + s_2 = 60$.

$$s_1 = v_1 t = 7t$$
$$s_2 = v_2 t = 5t$$
$$s_1 + s_2 = 60$$
$$7t + 5t = 60$$
$$12t = 60$$
$$t = \frac{60}{12}$$
$$t = 5$$

They will meet after 5 hours.

55. The answer is: 121.50

$$V = a^3$$
$$1{,}728 = a^3$$
$$a = \sqrt[3]{1{,}728} = 12$$

$$A = 6a^2 = 6 \times 12^2 = 6 \times 144 = 864$$

The number of cans needed to paint the cube:

$$\frac{864}{32} = 27$$

The total cost:
$27 \times 4.50 = \$121.50$

56. The answer is: -1 or 1

The function is undefined when the numerator is equal to zero.

$$y = \frac{1}{x^4 - 1}$$

$$x^4 - 1 = 0$$

$$(x^2)^2 - 1 = 0$$

$$(x^2 - 1)(x^2 + 1) = 0$$

$$(x - 1)(x + 1)(x^2 + 1) = 0$$

$$x - 1 = 0 \Rightarrow x = 1$$

$$x + 1 = 0 \Rightarrow x = -1$$

$x^2 + 1 = 0 \Rightarrow x^2 = -1 \Rightarrow x = \pm\sqrt{-1} \Rightarrow$no solution

57. The answer is: 1.06

$$p = 6\%$$

$$x = 1 + \frac{p}{100} = 1 + \frac{6}{100} = 1 + 0.06 = 1.06$$

58. The answer is: 12

$$2{,}200 \times (0.94)^t < 1{,}100$$

$$0.94^t < \frac{1{,}100}{2{,}200}$$

$$0.94^t < \frac{1}{2}$$

$$\log 0.94^t < \log\frac{1}{2}$$

$$t \log 0.94 < \log 1 - \log 2$$

$$t \log 0.94 < 0 - \log 2$$

$$t \log 0.94 < -\log 2$$

Since $\log 0.94 < 0$ we must multiply inequality by -1 and change the inequality sign.
$-t \log 0.94 > \log 2$

$$t > \frac{\log 2}{-\log 0.94} \approx 11.2$$

Therefore, the number of employees will be halved after 12 years.

TEST 2

1. The answer is B.

   Let x be the price of 1 can of soft drink and y be the price of 1 slice of pizza.

   We now analyze the situations to write the equations:

   $4x + 5y = 12.00$ (1st equation)
   $6x + 8y = 21.25$ (2nd equation)

   Subtract the terms of the 1st equation from the terms of the 2nd equation to obtain:

   $2x + 3y = 9.25$

   Multiply 4 to both sides of the 3rd equation to obtain:

   $8x + 12y = 37.00$ Thus, 8 cans of soft drinks and 12 slices of pizza cost $37.00

2. The answer is A.

   John's equation: $(x-9)(x-7) = x^2 - 16x + 63 = 0$; the constant is wrong

   Dave's equation: $(x-7)(x-4) = x^2 - 11x + 28 = 0$; the middle term is wrong

   Therefore, the right equation is: $x^2 - 16x + 28 = 0$

3. The answer is B.

   Divide both sides of the equation by 2: $2e^{2x} - e^x = 0$

   Let $r = e^x$

   $2r^2 - r = 0$
   $r(2r - 1) = 0$ which means either:
   $r = 0$ OR $2r - 1 = 0 \rightarrow r = ½$

   But $r = e^x$
   $e^x = 0$ (impossible)
   $2e^x = 1 \rightarrow e^x = ½ \rightarrow x = \log_e 1/2 = -\log_e 2$

4. The answer is C.

   $$\frac{1}{\sqrt{10}-3} \times \frac{\sqrt{10}+3}{\sqrt{10}+3} = \frac{\sqrt{10}+3}{10-9} = \frac{\sqrt{10}+3}{1} = 3 + \sqrt{10}$$

   $x = 3$; $y = 1$

5. The answer is C.

$V = \pi r^2 h$
$h = 20/ \pi r^2$

$A = 2\pi r^2 + 2\pi rh = 2\pi r^2 + 2\pi r(20/ \pi r^2)$
$A = 2\pi r^2 + 40/r$

6. The answer is C.

We know that the standard quadratic equation can be written as: $(a - b)^2 = a^2 - 2ab + b^2$

Therefore,
$(\sqrt{8} - 8)^2 = 8 - 2(\sqrt{8})(8) + b^2$
$= (8 - 16\sqrt{8} + 64)$
$= 72 - 16\sqrt{8}$
$= 8(9 - 2\sqrt{8})$

7. The answer is A.

$\frac{\sin \alpha}{x+2} = \frac{\sin 30}{x}$

$\alpha = sin^{-1} (\frac{(x+2)\sin 30}{x}) = sin^{-1} (\frac{(x+2)}{2x})$

8. The answer is B.

x + 5 > 0
x > -5

9. The answer is A.

RA = 80t
RB = 100 – 50t

$r^2 = RA^2 + RB^2$ - 2*RA*RB* cos 60
$r^2 = (80t)^2 + (100 - 50t)^2 - 2\,(80t)(100 - 50t)\frac{1}{2}$
$r^2 = 6400t^2 + 10000 - 10000t + 2500t^2 - 8000t + 4000t^2$
$r^2 = 12900t^2 - 18000t + 10000$

$r = \sqrt{12900t^2 - 18000t + 10000}$

10. The answer is D.

$9x^3 + 18x^2 - 4x - 8 = 0$

$(9x^3 + 18x^2) - (4x - 8) = 0$ We can use the grouping method to factor this.

$9x^2(x + 2) - 4(-x + 2) = 0$

(x + 2) $(9x^2 - 4)$ = 0

(x + 2) (3x + 2) (3x – 2) = 0

So, $x = -2, x = -\frac{3}{2}, and\ x = \frac{3}{2}$

11. The answer is A.

$\frac{x^2-2x-8}{x^2-9x+20} = \frac{(x-4)(x+2)}{(x-5)(x-4)} = \frac{x+2}{x-5}$

12. The answer is C.

$\frac{x^2-9}{x^2+5x+6} \div \frac{3-x}{x+2} = \frac{x^2-9}{x^2+5x+6} * \frac{x+2}{3-x} = \frac{(x-3)(x+3)}{(x+3)(x+2)} * \frac{x+2}{3-x}$

$= \frac{x-3}{3-x} = \frac{x-3}{-(x-3)}$ = -1

13. The answer is B.

$\angle DBA = \pi - \frac{5\pi}{6} = \frac{\pi}{6}$

$\angle DAB = \pi - \frac{2\pi}{6} = \pi - \frac{\pi}{3} = \frac{2\pi}{3}$

14. The answer is A.

To convert radians to degrees, simply multiply the radians by $\frac{180}{\pi}$

$\frac{5\pi}{6} * \frac{180}{\pi}$ we can combine this,

$= \frac{900\pi}{6\pi}$ now, we can see that 6 can divide into 900

$= \frac{150\pi}{\pi}$ and, we can see that the π will cancel

$= 150°$

15. The answer is A.

$$\frac{(4x^2y^{-2})^4}{(8xy^3)^4} = \left(\frac{4x^2y^{-2}}{8xy^3}\right)^4 = \left(\frac{x^{2-1}}{2y^{3+2}}\right)^4 = \left(\frac{x}{2y^5}\right)^4 = \frac{x^4}{16y^{20}}$$

16. The answer is: 100

Let the width = x and length = x+30

x(x + 30) = 400
x^2 + 30x – 400 = 0
(x + 40)(x – 10) = 0
X = -40 or x = 10
X = -40 is impossible, so x = 10
Width = 10mm, L = 40mm

Perimeter = 2 (length + width) = 2(50) = 100mm

17. The answer is: 3400

This is a difference of squares, which has the form: $x^2 - y^2$ = (x - y) (x + y)
Therefore,
$(67)^2 - (33)^2$ = (67 - 33) (67 + 33) = 34 x 100 = 3400

18. The answer is: 0.17 or 1/6

$10^{2x} = 36$

$(10^x)^2 = (6)^2$

$10^x = 6$

$\frac{1}{10^x} = \frac{1}{6}$

$10^{-x} = \frac{1}{6}$

19. The answer is: -4

Solve for x:

$x = \frac{5}{4+K}$

The given equation has one solution for all real values of K not equal to -4

20. The answer is: 1.5 or 3/2

Determine the slopes of the 2 lines:

$y = \frac{3x+6}{M}$; Slope is $\frac{3}{M}$

$y = \frac{-(x+8)}{2}$; Slope is $-\frac{1}{2}$

For 2 lines to be perpendicular, the product of their slopes must be equal to -1.

Thus, we get: $\left(\frac{3}{M}\right) * \left(-\frac{1}{2}\right) = -1$

Solving for M, we get: $M = \frac{3}{2}$

21. The answer is C.

Bag 1:
120% of X = 120
1.2X = 120
X = 120/1.2
X = 100
Profit is 120 – 100 = $20

Bag 2:
80% of X = 120
0.8X = 120
X = 120/0.8
X = 150
Profit is 120 – 150 = -$30

Total Profit is $20 - $30 = -$10

22. The answer is A.

Let x and x + 40 be the speed of John from A to B and then from B to A.

Hence; the distance from A to B maybe expressed as 20x and the distance from B to A as 12(x+40)

The average speed = total distance / total time = (20x + 12(x+40)) / (20 + 12).

Consequently, the distance A to B is equal to the distance from B to A. Thus, 20x = 12(x+40) and solve for x will get X = 60 meters per minute. Then substitute x by 60 in the average speed formula will obtain:

Average speed = 75 meters per minute

23. The answer is B.

$x^2 - x(\alpha + \beta) + \alpha\beta = 0$

So, $\alpha\beta = -2$ and ($(\alpha + \beta) = -5$

$\alpha\beta + (\alpha + \beta) = -2 + (-5) = -7$

24. The answer is B.

Let x = side of the square

A = $x^2 = 100$
x = 10

Diameter of the circle is equal to the length of the diagonal (D) of the square.

$D^2 = x^2 + x^2 = 200$

A (circle) = $\frac{\pi D^2}{4} = \frac{200\pi}{4}$ = 157.08

25. The answer is A.

There are 39 cards that different suit from the first, with 51 cards left.
So, probability is:

P = $\frac{39}{51} = 0.76$

26. The answer is A.

P = $\frac{39}{51} * \frac{26}{50} * \frac{13}{49}$ = 0.105

27. The answer is A.

This problem is much more awesome than it seems. It's a great problem because it tests the understanding of several concepts: the distance formula, slope, coordinates, linear equation, and solving linear equations. We can use two methods to solve this question – one is short and one is long.

The short method is to use the distance of a point to a line formula:

The distance from a point (m,n) to the line Ax + By + C = 0 is given by

$$d = \frac{|Am + Bn + C|}{\sqrt{A^2 + B^2}}$$

This distance is always perpendicular and is the shortest distance.

So, let's first put the original equation into the form Ax + By + C = 0

5x – y + 2 = 0 and point (-2, 3)

Therefore, A is 5; B is -1; C is 2; m is -2; n is 3 → Let's plug in everything and solve.

D = $\frac{|(5*-2) + (-1*3) + 2|}{\sqrt{5^2 + (-1)^2}} = \frac{11}{\sqrt{26}}$

The long method involves getting the equation of the line from the point to the original line. Then you have to equate the two linear equations together, which would give you the x value of the point of intersection of the two lines. You would then need to plug that value into either equation to get the y coordinate. After this, you have to use the regular distance of a line formula to finally find the distance. This method is far too long and I wouldn't advise it for this sort of question unless you have 5 minutes to spare. Memorize the above formula and use it in this situation.

28. The answer is D.

Area of the sector:

$A = \frac{\theta}{2} r^2$

$60 = \frac{\theta}{2} 4^2$

$60 = 8\theta \rightarrow \theta = \frac{60}{8}$

Length of the arc = $r\theta = 4 * \frac{60}{8}$ = 30cm

29. The answer is B.

Let x = number of people with both high blood pressure and high level of cholesterol.
25 – x = number of people with high blood pressure only
35 – x = number of people with high level of cholesterol only

(25 – x) + (35 – x) + x = 40

x = 20 people

30. The answer is D.

Number of people with high blood pressure = 20 + 5 = 15

$\frac{25}{50}$ = 0.5

31. The answer is A.

Number of people with high level of cholesterol = 20 + 15 = 35

$\frac{35}{50}$ = 0.7

32. The answer is A.

P (chocolate) = $\frac{4}{12} * \frac{3}{11} = \frac{12}{132} = 0.09$

33. The answer is C.

P (same flavor) = 3 * $\frac{12}{132} = \frac{36}{132} = 0.27$

34. The answer is C.

P (different flavor) = 1 – 0.27 = 0.73

35. The answer is C.

Let T be the price of 1 tea and B be the price of 1 biscuit.

Now, 3 teas and 4 biscuits cost \$10.05

⇨ $3T + 4B = 10.05$

And, 5 teas and 7 biscuits costs \$17.15

⇨ $5T + 7B = 17.15$

Subtract the terms of the first equation from the terms of the second equation to obtain

⇨ $2T + 3B = 7.10$

Multiply by 2, all terms of the last equation to obtain

⇨ $4T + 6B = 14.2$

Thus, 4 teas and 6 biscuits cost \$14.2.

36. The answer is C.

The standard deviation for any set, is how far the other values are from the mean.

For example, let's take the set: 1, 3, 5

The mean is 3 and the standard deviation is 2.

Now let's add 5 to each term in the set: 6, 8, 10

The mean is 8 but the standard deviation is still the same, 2.

37. The answer is B.

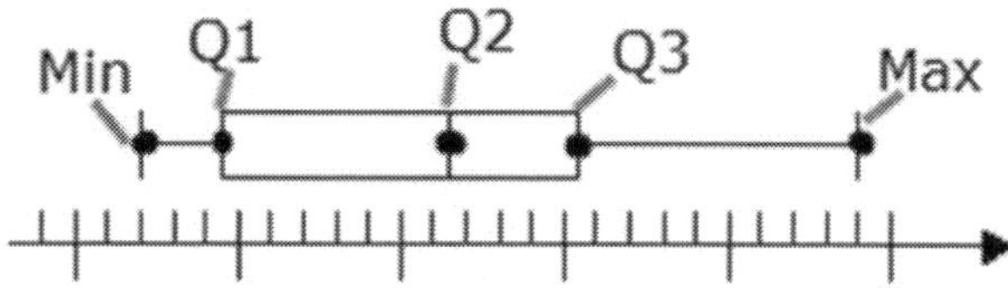

For a given set of data, in order to create a box-and-whisker plot, first you need to arrange the data in order from least to greatest.

Q2 is calculated first and is the median value of the entire set of ordered data.

Q1 is the median of the first half of the set of ordered data.

Q3 is the median of the second half of the set of ordered data.

The Min value (left whisker) is the lowest value in the set of ordered data.

The Max value (right whisker) is the greatest value in the set of ordered data.

38. The answer is B.

Arithmetic sequence:

$T_{15} = 3 + (14 * 2) = 31$

39. The answer is A.

$S_{15} = \frac{15}{2}(3 + T_{15}) = 7.5\ (3 + 31) = 255$ tiles

40. The answer is C.

We want $\frac{n}{2}(3 + T_n) = 200$

Where $T_n = 3 + 2\ (n - 1) = 2n + 1$

$\frac{n}{2}(3 + 2n + 1) = 200$

$\frac{n}{2}(2n + 4) = 200$

$n(n + 2) = 200$

$n^2 + 2n - 200 = 0$

$$n = \frac{-2 \pm \sqrt{2^2 - 4(1)(-200)}}{2(1)} = 13.177 \text{ or } -15.177$$

But number of tiles cannot be negative so Sam can make 13 complete rows.

41. The answer is A.

If series, consider one resistor as x, then the other is 20-x

If parallel, 1/5 = 1/x + 1/(20-x)

$$\frac{1}{5} = \frac{(20 - x) + x}{x\,(20 - x)} = \frac{20}{20x - x^2}$$

$x^2 - 20x + 100 = 0$; If $a\,x^2 + bx + c = 0$

From quadratic formula: $x = \frac{-b \pm \sqrt{b^2 - 4ac}}{2a} = \frac{20 \pm \sqrt{400 - 400}}{2} = 10$

a = 1 ; b = -20 ; c = 100

So, both resistors are 10 Ohms

42. The answer is A.

The left vertex of the triangle has coordinates (0,0).

The right vertex of the triangle corresponds with the x-intercept of the line y = -2x+3, set y = 0 to obtain x = 3/2. Thus, right vertex has coordinates (3/2,0).

The top vertex is the point of intersection of the two lines y = x and y = -2x+3.

Combining the equations will get x = -2x+3 or 3x = 3 or x =1. Thus top vertex is (1, 1)

Area of triangle = $\frac{1}{2}\ bh = \frac{1}{2}\left(\frac{3}{2}\right)(1) = \frac{3}{4}$

43. The answer is C.
    At rest, x = 0
    10 – 2t =0
    t = 10/2 = 5 seconds

44. The answer is A.

    Mean of data set Z = $\frac{1+5+9+12+8}{5}$ = 7

45. The answer is A.

    P (not win) = $\left(1-\frac{1}{5}\right)*\left(1-\frac{2}{3}\right) = \frac{4}{5}*\frac{1}{3} = \frac{4}{15} = 0.27$

46. The answer is B.

47. The answer is D.

    P (Sat wet) = $\left(\frac{1}{2}*\frac{1}{6}\right) + \left(\frac{1}{2}*\frac{1}{2}\right) = \frac{1}{12}+\frac{1}{4} = \frac{1+3}{12}$ = 0.33

48. The answer is A.

    P (Both Sat & Sun dry) = $\left(\frac{1}{2}*\frac{5}{6}*\frac{1}{2}\right) + \left(\frac{1}{2}*\frac{1}{2}*\frac{1}{2}\right) = \frac{5}{24}+\frac{1}{8} = \frac{5+3}{24} = 0.33$

49. The answer is B.

    P (at least Sat or Sun wet) = $1 - P$ (both dry) = 1 – 0.33 = 0.67

50. The answer is B.

    Fishing licenses sold in Ingram County = 1500

Fishing licenses sold in Lenawee County = 4500

Their ratio = 1500:4500

Ratio in the reduced form = 5:9

51. The answer is: 20

Distance = Rate × Time

Deepika can walk 3600 feet (1200 yards) in 10 minutes (600 seconds).

Therefore, her walking Rate = $\frac{Distance}{Time} = \frac{1200}{600}$ = 2 yards per second.

In 10 seconds, she can walk 10 x 2 = 20 yards.

52. The answer is: 0.63

P (Cheer | Glee) = $\frac{P\ (Glee\ and\ Cheer\ dance)}{P\ (Glee)} = \frac{0.22}{0.35} = 0.63$

53. The answer is: 0.38 or 3/8

P (fail) = $\frac{15}{40} = \frac{3}{8}$ = 0.38

54. The answer is: 128

$h = -16t^2 + 64t + 80 == -16(3)^2 + 64(3) + 80$ = 128m

55. The answer is: 144

To find the maximum height, we need to put the quadratic formula in vertex form:

$$h = -16t^2 + 64t + 80$$
$$h = -16(t^2 - 4t - 5)$$
$$h = -16((t-2)^2 - 9)$$
$$h = -16(t-2)^2 + 144$$

So, the answer is 144.

56. The answer is: 5

When the ball hit the ground h =0

$$-16t^2 + 64t + 80 = 0$$
$$t^2 - 4t - 5 = 0$$
$$(t-5)(t+1) = 0$$

t = 5 or t = -1 but time cannot be negative so the time = 5 seconds.

57. The answer is: 10/3 or 3.33

A (triangle) = $\frac{1}{2}$ (BC)(AN) = $\frac{1}{2}$ (AC)(BM)

BM = $\frac{(BC)(AN)}{AC} = \frac{(5)(4)}{6} = \frac{20}{6} = \frac{10}{3} = 3.33$

58. The answer is: 3.65

AM = AC – MC = 6 – 4.5 = 1.5

$(AB)^2 = (AM)^2 + (BM)^2 = (1.5)^2 + (3.33)^2$

$AB = \sqrt{2.25 + 11.09}$ = 3.65

TEST 3

1. The answer is B.

$$3(x+k)-x=2k \wedge k=-1$$
$$3\big(x+(-1)\big)-x=2(-1)$$
$$3(x-1)-x=-2$$
$$3x-3-x=-2$$
$$2x=3-2$$
$$2x=1$$
$$x=\frac{1}{2}$$

$$4-2x=4-2\times\frac{1}{2}=4-1=3$$

2. The answer is B.

$$(4+3i)(3-5i)=12-20i+9i-15i^2=12-11i-15(-1)=$$
$$=12-11i+15=27-11i$$

3. The answer is C.

Each cow has 4 legs, and each chicken has 2 legs. The total number of legs of cows is $4m$, and the total number of legs of chickens is $2n$. Therefore, the total number of legs of cows and chickens is $4m+2n=2(2m+n)$.

4. The answer is A.

C – the total cost of taxi
3 – the cost of every additional mile passed
n – the number of miles passed
5 – the cost of start

5. The answer is C.

$$(3x-2)(x^2+2x-1)=3x^3+6x^2-3x-2x^2-4x+2=3x^3+4x^2-7x+2$$

6. The answer is B.

After 1st year the profit of the company is $P=100{,}000-34{,}000\times 1=66{,}000$.
After 2nd year the profit of the company is $P=100{,}000-34{,}000\times 2=32{,}000$.
After 3rd year the profit of the company is $P=100{,}000-34{,}000\times 3=-2{,}000$.
The profit in the first 2 years is positive, and after that it is negative. Therefore, company doesn't make profit each year.

7. The answer is D.

$$F = \frac{GMm}{r^2}$$
$$Fr^2 = GMm$$
$$r^2 = \frac{GMm}{F}$$
$$r = \sqrt{\frac{GMm}{F}}$$

8. The answer is C.

$$2a + b = 5$$
$$b = 5 - 2a$$

$$\frac{a}{2b - 10} = \frac{a}{2(5 - 2a) - 10} = \frac{a}{10 - 4a - 10} = \frac{a}{-4a} = -\frac{1}{4}$$

9. The answer is A.

$$4x - 5y = -23$$
$$3x + 2y = 0$$

$$12x - 15y = -69$$
$$-12x - 8y = 0$$

$$12x - 15y - 12x - 8y = -69 + 0$$
$$-23y = -69$$
$$y = \frac{-69}{-23} = 3$$

$$3x + 2y = 0$$
$$3x + 2 \times 3 = 0$$
$$3x + 6 = 0$$
$$3x = -6$$
$$x = -\frac{6}{3} = -2$$

10. The answer is D.

$f(3) = 2 \Leftrightarrow 2 = a \times 3^2 - 3 \times 3 + 2 \Leftrightarrow 2 = 9a - 9 + 2 \Leftrightarrow 2 + 9 - 2 = 9a \Leftrightarrow$
$\Leftrightarrow 9 = 9a \Leftrightarrow a = 1$
$f(-3) = 1(-3)^2 - 3(-3) + 2 = 9 + 9 + 2 = 20$

11. The answer is B.

$m = n$
$7 + 0.5h = 9 + 0.25h$
$0.5h - 0.25h = 9 - 7$
$0.25h = 2$
$$h = \frac{2}{0.25} = \frac{200}{25} = 8$$

12. The answer is A.

The points which lies on x or y-axis cannot lie on a line which passes through the origin. The point (-2,0) lies on x-axis. Therefore, it cannot lie on a line which passes through the origin.

13. The answer is C

$$\frac{1}{1 - \frac{1}{x}} = \frac{1}{\frac{x}{x} - \frac{1}{x}} = \frac{1}{\frac{x-1}{x}} = \frac{x}{x-1}$$

14. The answer is D.

$$\frac{9^x}{3^y} = \frac{(3^2)^x}{3^y} = \frac{3^{2x}}{3^y} = 3^{2x-y} = 3^4 = 81$$

15. The answer is A.

$(ax + b)(2x - 1) = 10x^2 + cx - b$
$2ax^2 - ax + 2bx - b = 10x^2 + cx - b$
$2ax^2 + (2b - a)x - b = 10x^2 + cx - b$

$2a = 10$
$a = 5$

$a + b = 8$
$b = 8 - a = 8 - 5 = 3$

$2b - a = c$
$c = 2b - a = 2 \times 3 - 5 = 6 - 5 = 1$

16. The answer is: 8

$x^2 - 5x - 24 = 0$

$a = 1, b = -5, c = -24$

$$x_{1,2} = \frac{-b \pm \sqrt{b^2 - 4ac}}{2a} = \frac{-(-5) \pm \sqrt{(-5)^2 - 4 \times 1 \times (-24)}}{2 \times 1} = \frac{5 \pm \sqrt{25 + 96}}{2} =$$

$$= \frac{5 \pm \sqrt{121}}{2} = \frac{5 \pm 11}{2}$$

$$x_1 = \frac{5 + 11}{2} = \frac{16}{2} = 8$$

$$x_2 = \frac{5 - 11}{2} = \frac{-6}{2} = -3$$

$x > 0 \Longrightarrow x = 8$

17. The answer is: $\frac{49}{3}$

Triangle ABC: $a_1 = 3, b_1 = 6, c_1 = 7$
Similar triangle: $a_2 = 7, b_2 =?, c_2 =?$
The longest side in the similar triangle is c_2.

$$\frac{a_1}{a_2} = \frac{c_1}{c_2}$$
$$\frac{3}{7} = \frac{7}{c_2}$$
$$3c_2 = 7 \times 7$$
$$c_2 = \frac{49}{3}$$

18. The answer is: 3

$2x + 6 = 3y$
$\frac{y}{2} + 1 = x$

$2x - 3y = -6$
$2 \times \frac{y}{2} + 2 \times 1 = 2x$

$2x - 3y = -6$
$y + 2 = 2x$

$2x - 3y = -6$

$-2x + y = -2$

$2x - 3y = -6$
$-6x + 3y = -6$

$2x - 3y - 6x + 3y = -6 - 6$
$-4x = -12$
$x = 3$

19. The answer is: $\frac{12}{5}$

$\sin^2 x + \cos^2 x = 1$

$$\sin^2 x = 1 - \cos^2 x = 1 - \left(\frac{5}{13}\right)^2 = 1 - \frac{25}{169} = \frac{169}{169} - \frac{25}{169} = \frac{144}{169}$$

$$\sin x = \sqrt{\frac{144}{169}} = \frac{12}{13}$$

$$\tan x = \frac{\sin x}{\cos x} = \frac{\frac{12}{13}}{\frac{5}{13}} = \frac{12 \times 13}{5 \times 13} = \frac{12}{5}$$

20. The answer is: 36

$a = 4\sqrt{3}$
$a\sqrt{3} = 2\sqrt{x}$
$4\sqrt{3}\sqrt{3} = 2\sqrt{x}$
$4 \times 3 = 2\sqrt{x}$
$12 = 2\sqrt{x}$
$\sqrt{x} = \frac{12}{2}$
$\sqrt{x} = 6$
$\left(\sqrt{x}\right)^2 = 6^2$
$x = 36$

21. The answer is B.

Minute	0	1	2	3	4
Speed	0	10	20	30	40

$$\{Average\ Speed\} = \frac{0 + 10 + 20 + 30 + 40}{5} = \frac{100}{5} = 20$$

22. The answer is D.

The equation of line which passes through the point is $y = kx + n$. Since a line passes through the point (12,-4) and intersects y-axis at 4 we have

$$x = 12, y = -4, n = 4$$
$$y = kx + n$$
$$-4 = k \times 12 + 4$$
$$-4 - 4 = 12k$$
$$-8 = 12k$$
$$k = -\frac{8}{12} = -\frac{2}{3}$$

The point in which a line intersects x-axis has coordinates (x,0)

$$y = kx + n$$
$$0 = -\frac{2}{3}x + 4$$
$$\frac{2}{3}x = 4$$
$$x = 4 \div \frac{2}{3} = 4 \times \frac{3}{2} = 2 \times 3 = 6$$

Therefore, the x-intercept of a line is the point (6,0).

23. The answer is B.

$$\sphericalangle DEC = \sphericalangle AEB = 81^o$$
$$\sphericalangle DEC + \alpha + 2\alpha = 180^o$$
$$81^o + 3\alpha = 180^o$$
$$3\alpha = 180^o - 81^o$$
$$3\alpha = 99^o$$
$$\alpha = 33^o$$
$$\sphericalangle BAE = \sphericalangle CDE \Rightarrow x^o = 2\alpha = 2 \times 33^o = 66^o$$

24. The answer is C.

$$\frac{3x-2}{4} + 2 = 3$$
$$4 \times \frac{3x-2}{4} + 4 \times 2 = 4 \times 3$$
$$3x - 2 + 8 = 12$$
$$3x + 6 = 12$$
$$3x = 6$$
$$x = 2$$

$$3 - 2x = 3 - 2 \times 2 = 3 - 4 = -1$$

25. The answer is B.

A graph with a strong negative association between *x* and *y* would have the points on the graph closely aligned with a line that has a negative slope. Of the four graphs, the points on graph B are most closely aligned with a line with a negative slope.

26. The answer is C.

$4\ quarts = 16\ cups \Longrightarrow 1\ quart = 4\ cups \Longrightarrow 3\ quarts = (3 \times 4)\ cups = 12\ cups$

27. The answer is C.

The sum of citizens in all towns on the graph is $8 + 3 + 6 + 7 + 4 = 28$.

$$\frac{280{,}000}{28} = 10{,}000$$

Therefore, an appropriate label for the vertical axis of the graph is ten thousands.

28. The answer is B.

$$|x - 2| < 3$$
$$-3 < x - 2 < 3$$
$$-3 + 2 < x - 2 + 2 < 3 + 2$$
$$-1 < x < 5$$

29. The answer is D.

$$P = \frac{20}{20 + R}$$
$$(20 + R)P = (20 + R)\frac{20}{20 + R}$$
$$(20 + R)P = 20$$
$$20P + RP = 20$$
$$RP = 20 - 20P$$
$$R = \frac{20 - 20P}{P}$$
$$R = \frac{20(1 - P)}{P}$$

30. The answer is A.

If the probability of picking a red apple is 0.2, then the probability of picking a green apple is $1 - 0.2 = 0.8$. Use the formula for the probability of picking a green apple from the bag.

$$P = \frac{20}{20 + R}$$
$$0.8 = \frac{20}{20 + R}$$
$$8 = \frac{200}{20 + R}$$
$$8(20 + R) = 200$$
$$160 + 8R = 200$$
$$8R = 200 - 160$$
$$8R = 40$$
$$R = 5$$

31. The answer is D.

$$\frac{2x}{3} - 1 < \frac{1}{3} + \frac{x}{2}$$
$$6 \times \frac{2x}{3} - 6 \times 1 < 6 \times \frac{1}{3} + 6 \times \frac{x}{2}$$
$$2 \times 2x - 6 < 2 \times 1 + 3x$$
$$4x - 6 < 2 + 3x$$
$$4x - 3x < 2 + 6$$
$$x < 8$$

32. The answer is C.

The following numbers appear in the graph: 5, 2, 3, 5, 3, 5, 7.
Median is the middle value of sorted data: 2, 3, 3, 5, 5, 5, 7. Therefore it is 5.

33. The answer is C.

$$\frac{\{Number\ of\ male\ cats\}}{\{Total\ number\ of\ cats\}} \times 100\% = \frac{6}{24} \times 100\% = 25\%$$

34. The answer is B.

The range is the difference between maximum and minimum value.

For all 4 rows:
$\{max\ value\} = 45$
$\{min\ value\} = 5$
$range = \{max\ value\} - \{min\ value\} = 45 - 5 = 40$

When you omit last row:
$\{max\ value\} = 45$
$\{min\ value\} = 7$
$range = \{max\ value\} - \{min\ value\} = 45 - 7 = 38$

$difference = 40 - 38 = 2$

35. The answer is D.

When the car passes 100 kilometers, the level of gas drops from 50 liters to 44 liters. So, the car needs 6 liters of gas to pass 100 kilometers. Therefore, the car needs 12 liters to pass 200 kilometers.

36. The answer is C.

When the car passes 100 kilometers, the level of gas drops from 50 liters to 44 liters. So, the car needs 6 liters of gas to pass 100 kilometers, and 3 liters to pass 50 kilometers. In order to pass 350 kilometers, car needs $3 \times 6 + 3 = 21$ liters. So, the level og gas in the tank after 350 kilometers passed is $50 - 21 = 29$ liters.

37. The answer is C.

The range is the difference between maximum and minimum value. The maximum point is the highest point, and the minimum point is the lowest point. According to graph, the coordinates of maximum point are (-2,4), and the coordinates of the minimum point are (3,-2). The y-coordinate of the maximum point is 4, and the
y-coordinate of the minimum point is -2. Therefore, the range of y is $-2 < y < 4$.

38. The answer is A.

$(1, -2) \Rightarrow x = 1, y = -2$
$-2x > b + 3y \Rightarrow -2 \times 1 > b + 3(-2) \Rightarrow -2 > b - 6 \Rightarrow -2 + 6 > b \Rightarrow 4 > b$
$5x - a < 2y \Rightarrow 5 \times 1 - a < 2(-2) \Rightarrow 5 - a < -4 \Rightarrow 5 + 4 < a \Rightarrow 9 < a$

$b < 4 \wedge a > 9 \Rightarrow a > b$

39. The answer is C.

$\frac{224\ liters}{2\ liters} = 112$ bottles of coke
x – number of 4-packs
y – number of 6-packs

$x + y = 21$

$4x + 6y = 112$

$x = 21 - y$
$4(21 - y) + 6y = 112$
$84 - 4y + 6y = 112$
$2y = 112 - 84$
$2y = 28$
$y = \frac{28}{2} = 14$

40. The answer is B.

n – the initial price of shirt
$n \times 1.06 \times 0.96 = m \Rightarrow n = \frac{m}{1.06 \times 0.96}$

41. The answer is B.

Years of experience of employees

	Less than 10	Between 10 and 20	Between 20 and 30	More than 30	Total
Males	12	14	8	6	40
Females	6	24	16	4	50
Total	18	38	24	10	90

There are $16 + 4 = 20$ employees with more than 20 years of experience. We choose at random from 90 employees.
$\frac{20}{90} = \frac{2}{9}$

42. The answer is D.

Number of students at Faculty of Natural Sciences and Mathematics

Department	Year			
	2010	2011	2012	2013
Math	120	90	110	86
Physics	86	90	96	108
Biology	94	76	88	92
Chemistry	108	120	115	103

$$\frac{86 + 90 + 96 + 108}{4} = \frac{380}{4} = 95$$

43. The answer is A.

Number of students at Faculty of Natural Sciences and Mathematics

Department	Year				
	2010	2011	2012	2013	2014
Math	120	90	110	86	
Physics	86	90	96	108	
Biology	94	76	88	92	
Chemistry	108	120	115	103	x

$$\frac{108 + 120 + 115 + 103 + x}{5} = 110$$

$$\frac{446 + x}{5} = 110$$

$$446 + x = 5 \times 110$$

$$446 + x = 550$$
$$x = 550 - 446$$
$$x = 104$$

44. The answer is B.

The equation of the circle is $(x-p)^2 + (y-q)^2 = r^2$, where the center of the circle is $C(p,q)$ and radius is r.

$$C(-1,2) \Rightarrow p = -1, q = 2$$

$$r = d(C,P)$$
$$C(-1,2) \Rightarrow x_1 = -1, y_1 = 2$$
$$P(1,1) \Rightarrow x_2 = 1, y_2 = 1$$
$$r = d(C,P) = \sqrt{(x_2 - x_1)^2 + (y_2 - y_1)^2} = \sqrt{\left(1-(-1)\right)^2 + (1-2)^2} =$$
$$= \sqrt{(1+1)^2 + (1-2)^2} = \sqrt{2^2 + (-1)^2} = \sqrt{4+1} = \sqrt{5}$$

$$(x-p)^2 + (y-q)^2 = r^2$$
$$\left(x-(-1)\right)^2 + (y-2)^2 = \sqrt{5}^2$$
$$(x+1)^2 + (y-2)^2 = 5$$

45. The answer is B.

$$P = -2$$

$$P = \frac{1}{4}t^2 + t - 5$$

$-2 = \frac{1}{4}t^2 + t - 5$

$-2 \times 4 = 4 \times \frac{1}{4}t^2 + 4t - 4 \times 5$

$-8 = t^2 + 4t - 20$

$t^2 + 4t - 20 + 8 = 0$

$t^2 + 4t - 12 = 0$

$a = 1, b = 4, c = -12$

$$t_{1,2} = \frac{-b \pm \sqrt{b^2 - 4ac}}{2a} = \frac{-4 \pm \sqrt{4^2 - 4 \times 1 \times (-12)}}{2 \times 1} = \frac{-4 \pm \sqrt{16 + 48}}{2} =$$

$$= \frac{-4 \pm \sqrt{64}}{2} = \frac{-4 \pm 8}{2}$$

$$t_1 = \frac{-4 + 8}{2} = \frac{4}{2} = 2$$

$$t_2 = \frac{-4 - 8}{2} = \frac{-12}{2} = -6$$

Number of years must be positive. Therefore $t = 2$. The company had loss of $2,000,000 at the end of 2nd year.

46. The answer is A.

g – number of girls
b – number of boys

$b = g + 25\%g = g + \frac{25}{100}g = g + 0.25g = 1.25g$
$g + b = 27$
$g + 1.25g = 27$
$2.25g = 27$
$g = \frac{27}{2.25} = \frac{2,700}{225} = \frac{540}{45} = \frac{108}{9} = 12$

47. The answer is D.

Number of girls in a sample: $8 + 5 + 12 + 7 + 18 = 50$
Number of students in a sample: $5 \times 25 = 125$
Number of students in the school: $8 \times 4 \times 25 = 800$

$$\frac{\{\text{Number of girls in a sample}\}}{\{\text{Number of students in a sample}\}} = \frac{\{\text{Number of girls in the school}\}}{\{\text{Number of students in the school}\}}$$

$50: 125 = x: 800$

$125x = 50 \times 800$

$x = \frac{50 \times 800}{125} = \frac{2 \times 800}{5} = 2 \times 160 = 320$

48. The answer is D.

Solve the inequality $y \leq 3x + 5$ graphically.

x	-1	-2
y	2	-1

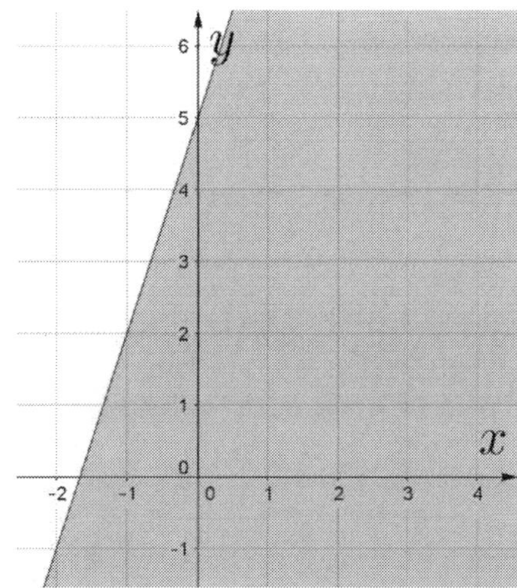

All points in the IV quadrant are the solutions to the inequality.

49. The answer is A.

$q(x)$ - quotient of division of two polynomials $a(x)$ and $b(x)$
r – the rest

$\frac{a(x)}{b(x)} = q(x) + \frac{r}{b(x)}$

$\frac{a(x)}{x-2} = q(x) + \frac{5}{x-2}$

$(x-2)\frac{a(x)}{x-2} = (x-2)q(x) + (x-2)\frac{5}{x-2}$

$a(x) = (x-2)q(x) + 5$

$a(2) = (2-2)q(2) + 5$

$a(2) = 0 + 5 = 5$

$a(2) - 5 = 5 - 5 = 0$
Therefore, statement $a(2) - 5 = 0$ is true.

50. The answer is A.

The equation of parabola is $y = a(x - x_1)(x - x_2)$, where x_1 and x_2 are x-intercepts.
$A(-1,0)$ and $B(3,0) \Rightarrow x_1 = -1, x_2 = 3$

$y = a(x - x_1)(x - x_2)$
$y = a(x - (-1))(x - 3)$
$y = a(x + 1)(x - 3)$

$V(1,4) \Rightarrow x = 1, y = 4$
$y = a(x + 1)(x - 3)$
$4 = a(1 + 1)(1 - 3)$
$4 = a \times 2 \times (-2)$
$4 = -4a$
$a = -1$

$y = -1(x + 1)(x - 3)$
$y = -(x^2 - 3x + x - 3)$
$y = -(x^2 - 2x - 3)$
$y = -x^2 + 2x + 3$

51. The answer is: 2, 3, or 4

Alex needs at most $\frac{12}{3} = 4$ hours, and at least $\frac{12}{6} = 2$ hours to create 12 questions. Therefore, any number between 2 and 4, inclusive, is a solution.

52. The answer is: 1 or 2

x – starting number
$\frac{x - 18}{3} + 8 > x$
$3 \times \frac{x - 18}{3} + 3 \times 8 > 3x$
$x - 18 + 24 > 3x$
$x + 6 > 3x$
$6 > 3x - x$
$6 > 2x$
$2x < 6$

$$x < \frac{6}{2}$$
$$x < 3$$

53. The answer is: 75

The number of employees in 2011: 30.
The number of employees in 2014: 40.

$$\frac{30}{40} \times 100\% = \frac{3}{4} \times 100\% = 0.75 \times 100\% = 75\%$$

54. The answer is: 760

$$\{5\ days\} \times \{4\ hours\} \times \$30 + \{2\ days\} \times \{2\ hours\} \times \$40 = \$600 + \$160 =$$
$$= \$760$$

55. The answer is: 602.88

$$d = 12$$
$$2r = 12$$
$$r = 6$$

$$V = r^2\pi h$$
$$h = \frac{V}{r^2\pi} = \frac{360\pi}{6^2\pi} = \frac{360}{36} = 10$$

$$A = 2r\pi(r + h) = 2 \times 6\pi(6 + 10) = 12\pi \times 16 = 192\pi \approx 192 \times 3.14 = 602.88$$

56. The answer is: $-\frac{16}{3}$

The intersection point has coordinates $(x, 0)$.
$y = x^2 + 8x - 3k$
$0 = x^2 + 8x - 3k$
In order to have 1 solution for the quadratic equation above, discriminant must be equal to zero.
$a = 1, b = 8, c = -3k$
$D = b^2 - 4ac = 8^2 - 4 \times 1 \times (-3k) = 64 + 12k$
$D = 0$
$64 + 12k = 0$
$12k = -64$

$$k = -\frac{64}{12} = -\frac{32}{6} = -\frac{16}{3}$$

57. The answer is: 1

In that case the number of employees is always 2,200. So, the expression $(x)^t$ must be equal to 1. It is equal to 1, when the base of the exponent is 1. Therefore, $x = 1$.

58. The answer is: 2

$2{,}200 \times (0.94)^t < 2{,}000$
$0.94^t < \dfrac{2{,}000}{2{,}200}$
$0.94^t < \dfrac{10}{11}$
$\log 0.94^t < \log\dfrac{10}{11}$
$t\log 0.94 < \log 10 - \log 11$
Since $\log 0.94 < 0$ we must multiply inequality by -1 and change the inequality sign.
$-t\log 0.94 > -(\log 10 - \log 11)$
$-t\log 0.94 > \log 11 - \log 10$

$$t > \frac{\log 11 - \log 10}{-\log 0.94} = \frac{\log 10 - \log 11}{\log 0.94} = \frac{1 - \log 11}{\log 0.94} \approx 1.54$$

Therefore, the number of employees will be less than 2,000 after 2 years.

TEST 4

1. The answer is B.

The solution $x = 1, y = -\frac{3}{2}$ satisfies the equation. Hence, substituting the solution in the equation, we get

$3 * 1 + \alpha * \left(-\frac{3}{2}\right) = -3$

$3 - \frac{3\alpha}{2} = -3$

$\frac{3\alpha}{2} = 6$, which gives $\alpha = 4$

2. The answer is A.

The graph of a linear function is a line and the graph of a quadratic function is a parabola. A line and a parabola can intersect in one, two or no points.

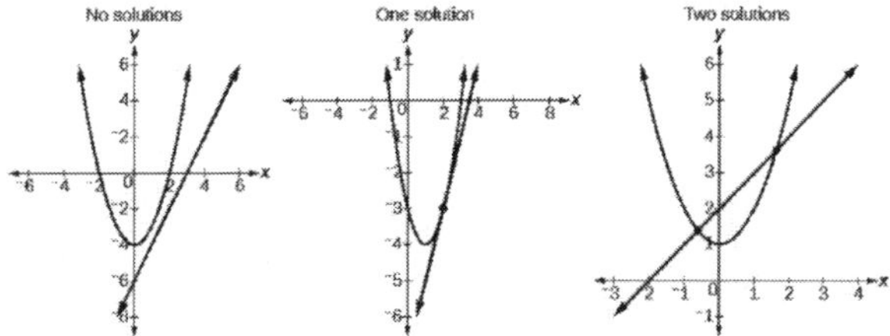

3. The answer is B.

It is given that $K_{John} = 2 * K_{Josh}$

Josh's pay = $= \$500 + K_{Josh} * Hours$

Twice Josh's pay = $2 * (\$500 + K_{Josh} * Hours) = \$1000 + 2 * K_{Josh} * Hours$

John's pay $= \$500 + K_{John} * Hours$ = $\$500 + 2 * K_{Josh} * Hours$ which is less than twice Josh's pay.

4. The answer is C.

We check that 4 does not satisfy the given equation.

5. The answer is A.

Since triangles ABC and PQR are similar we have $\frac{AB}{PQ} = \frac{BC}{QR} = \frac{CA}{RP}$.

Using the first part of the equality, we have $\frac{AB}{BC} = \frac{PQ}{QR}$

Since it is given that $\frac{AB}{BC} = 2$, we get PQ = 2QR

6. The answer is C.

Since new members are accepted only when old members leave, if n new members have been inducted then $\frac{n}{2}$ members should have left. Hence total membership should be

$$320 + n - \frac{n}{2} = 320 + \frac{n}{2}$$

7. The answer is A.

Sum of roots of the equation = $-\frac{-9}{2} = \frac{9}{2}$

If one of the values is 5, the other should be $\frac{9}{2} - 5 = -\frac{1}{2} = -0.$

8. The answer is D.

Consider, the equations $x + 3y = 4$ and $2x + y = 3$. The only solution of the equations is $x = 1, y = 1$. This value does not satisfy the last equation $x - y = 3$. Hence, the number of solutions of the system is zero.

9. The answer is A.

We can write $q(x) = x^2 - 2x + 5 = (x-1)^2 + 4$
Note that $(x-1)^2 \geq 0$ for all values of x. Hence, $(x-1)^2 + 4$ is always positive (and, in fact, ≥ 4)

10. The answer is B.

$= \frac{x+3}{x+1} + \frac{x+1}{1-x}$

$= \frac{(x+3)(1-x)+(x+1)(x+1)}{(x+1)(1-x)}$ (Taking a common denominator)

$= \frac{(-x^2+x-3x+3)+(x^2+2x+1)}{(x+1)(1-x)}$ (Expanding the terms in the numerator)

$= \frac{4}{(x+1)(1-x)} = \frac{4}{1-x^2} = -\frac{4}{x^2-1}$

11. The answer is C.

When $x > \frac{1}{2}$,

$$|x+1| = x+1 \text{ (since } x+1 \text{ is positive for } x > \tfrac{1}{2})$$

and

$$|1-2x| = -(1-2x) \ \ ((1-2x) \text{ is negative for } x > \tfrac{1}{2})$$

Hence,

$$m(x) = |x+1| + |1-2x|$$
$$= (x+1) - (1-2x)$$
$$= 3x$$

12. The answer is C.

$$= \frac{1+i}{1-i} + \frac{1-i}{1+i}$$
$$= \frac{(1+i)^2 + (1-i)^2}{(1-i)(1+i)}$$
$$= \frac{(1+i^2+2i) + (1+i^2-2i)}{1-i^2}$$
$$= \frac{(1-1+2i) + (1-1-2i)}{1-(-1)} = \frac{0}{2} = 0$$

13. The answer is C.

Since $f(g(1)) = 0$ and $g(1) = 3.3$, we have $f(3.3) = 0$.

14. The answer is B.

$|x+1| < 2$ is solved as $-2 < x+1 < 2 \quad i.e. -3 < x < 1$ which has a length of 4 units on the real line.

$|2x-3| < 3$ is solved as $-3 < 2x-3 < 3 \quad i.e. 0 < 2x < 6 \quad i.e. \ 0 < x < 3$ which has a length of 3 units on the real line.

$|5x-4| < 15$ is solved as $-15 < 5x-5 < 15 \quad i.e. -10 < 5x < 20 \ \ i.e. -2 < x < 4$ which has a length of 6 units on the real line.

$|x+1| > 3$ is solved as $x+1 > 3 \ or \ \ x+1 < -3$. This gives two rays of infinite length.

15. The answer is B.

$q(1) = 1^2 + 2*1 = 3$
$q(\alpha) = \alpha^2 + 2\alpha$

$$q\left(\frac{1+\alpha}{2}\right)=\left(\frac{1+\alpha}{2}\right)^2+2*\frac{1+\alpha}{2}=(\frac{1}{4}+\frac{\alpha^2}{4}+\frac{\alpha}{2})+1+\alpha=\frac{5}{4}+\frac{3\alpha}{2}+\frac{\alpha^2}{4}$$

Hence, $q(1)+\ q(\alpha)-\ 2q\left(\frac{1+\alpha}{2}\right)=\ 3+\ \alpha^2+2\alpha-2*\left(\frac{5}{4}+\frac{3\alpha}{2}+\frac{\alpha^2}{4}\right)=\frac{1}{2}-\alpha+\frac{\alpha^2}{2}=\frac{1}{4}+$ $\left(\alpha-\frac{1}{2}\right)^2$, which is always greater than zero.

16. The answer is: 75°

Since AB = AC, ABC = BCA. Also BAC = 30°
Hence,
ABC + BCA + BAC = 180°
BCA + BCA + 30° = 180°
2BCA = 180° – 30° = 150° i.e. BCA = 75°

17. The answer is: 2

Expanding the left hand side the equation becomes,
$72+160t=392$
$160t=320$, which gives $t=2$

18. The answer is: 3200

If the number of females is x, then the number of males is $x-300$. The total population is 6100. Hence we have the equation,
$x+x-300=6100$ i.e. 2x – 300 = 6100 which when solved gives $x=3200$

19. The answer is: 9

The product is $x^3+x^2+4x^2+4x+5x+5=x^3+5x^2+\mathbf{9}x+5$

20. The answer is: 58

Note the expansion $(2a+3b)^2=4a^2+12ab+9b^2$.
Hence,
$4a^2+4a+9b^2+6b+12ab-5$
$=(4a^2+12ab+9b^2)+(4a+6b)-\ 5$ (moving terms around)
$=(2a+3b)^2+2(2a+3b)-\ 5$ (collecting terms)
$=(7)^2+2(7)-\ 5=49+14-5=58$

21. The answer is D.

March represents the lowest point on the graph.

22. The answer is A.

$$h(1+t) - h(1-t) = 3(1+t) + 7 - 3(1-t) - 7 = 6t$$

Hence, $\frac{h(1+t)-h(1-t)}{2t} = \frac{6t}{2t} = 3$

23. The answer is A.

Number of persons in Type A = 45
Number of persons in Group 1 that are of Type A is 14
The required conditional probability = $\frac{14}{45}$

24. The answer is B.

Number of persons in Group 1 who are not of Type A is 24 + 35 = 59
Number of persons in Group 1 that are of Type C is 35
The required conditional probability = $\frac{35}{59}$

25. The answer is B.

For $y = 0.33$, $100 - 3y = 100 - 0.99 = 99.01$.
Hence, $x = 99$ is an integer that satisfies the inequalities.
Since y cannot take the value 0, $x = 99$ is the largest integer value possible for x

26. The answer is A.

Rewriting the equations as

$$x + 2y = K$$

and

$$4x - my = 12$$

Hence, we have

$$\frac{1}{4} = \frac{2}{-m} = \frac{K}{12}$$

Solving we get, $m = -8$ and $K = 3$

27. The answer is D.

28. The answer is C.

The initial amount of diesel in the car is 60 liters. To drive x miles, an amount of diesel proportional to x is used up. So the amount of diesel left, after driving x miles, should look like $60 - constant * x$

29. The answer is B.

$y + 3x = 2$ implies $y = 2 - 3x$

Substituting for y in $x + y \geq 7$, we get

$x + (2 - 3x) \geq 7$

$2 - 2x \geq 7$

$-5 \geq 2x$ i.e. $x \leq -\frac{5}{2}$

30. The answer is D.

Density of A: $5g/cm^3$
Density of B: $\frac{35}{10} = 3.5g/cm^3$
Density of C: $\frac{40}{14} = 2.857g/cm^3$
Density of C < Density of B < Density of A

31. The answer is B.

$x = 1, x = -1$ are roots of the polynomial $(x^2 - 1)$ and hence also of $q(x)(x^2 - 1)$, It follows that $x = 1, x = -1$ should be roots of the equation $x^5 - ax + b$.
Substituting $x = 1$ in $x^5 - ax + b$ and setting it to zero we get,
$1^5 - a * 1 + b = 0\ i.e. a - b = 1$
Substituting $x = -1$ in $x^5 - ax + b$ and setting it to zero we get,
$(-1)^5 - a * (-1) + b = 0\ i.e. a + b = 1$
Solving the two equations simultaneously we get $a = 1, b = 0$

32. The answer is B.

Suppose her walking speed is w miles per minute. Then her biking speed is $4.5w$ miles per minute. The distance to the first station is $w * 15$. The distance to second station has two different expressions that are equal:

$$w * 15 + 3 = 4.5w * 12$$

Solving the above we get w = 1/13 i.e. a mile in 13 minutes.

33. The answer is A.

34. The answer is B.

$\sqrt{x + 1} = 1 - x$
Squaring both sides,
$x + 1 = x^2 - 2x + 1$
$x^2 - 3x = 0$

Which, gives x = 0 or x = 3.

Since we squared the equation while solving (which is not a reversible process), we have to check the solutions by substituting in the original equation.
We see that 0 is a solution while 3 is not.

35. The answer is D.

Let n denote the number of dolls. The total cloth available can be represented in two different ways that are equal

$$6n + 5 = 7(n - 3)$$

Solving the above, we get $n = 26$

36. The answer is D.

Product 1 has sales 4000 in all the countries. Hence, its average is 4000

Product 2 has sales 3000, 4000, 4000 and 5000 in the countries. Hence, it's average =

$\frac{3000+4000+4000+5000}{4} = 4000$

Product 3 has sales 1000, 3000, 4000 and 7000. Hence, it's average = $\frac{1000+3000+4000+7000}{4} = 3750$

37. The answer is C.

The sales of Product 1 is the same among the countries, hence there is no deviation.
Comparing sales of product 2 and product 3 we see that the sales numbers for product 3 deviate substantially more than that for product 1.

38. The answer is A.

Plan A after 5 years = $D\left(1 + \frac{2.5}{100}\right)^{5*4} = 1.64D$

Plan B after 5 years = $D\left(1 + \frac{4}{100}\right)^{5*2} = 1.48D$

39. The answer is A.

Let us consider a good of price $100.
Dealer x marks it up to 100 + 30% of 100 = $130.
He then provides a discount of 10% i.e. final value = 130 – 10% of 130 = 130 – 13 = $117.
Dealer Y marks it up to 100 + 35% of 100 = $135
He then provides a discount of 15% i.e. final value = 135 – 15% of 135 = 135 – 20.25 = $114.75

40. The answer is A.

Note that the volume of a cone is equal to the volume of a cylinder with the same base radius and with one-third height as that of the cone. This can be seen by writing the volume of a cone as

$$\pi r^2(\frac{1}{3}h)$$

Which is the same as the volume of a cylinder with base radius r and height $\frac{1}{3}h$

41. The answer is A.

Consider the point $(3,15)$ lying in the shaded region: The line $2x + y - 8 = 0$ divides the plane into two parts. Substituting in $2x + y - 8$, we get the value 13. Therefore, $2x + y \geq 8$ for the shaded region. Similarly, we see that $y - 3x \geq -9$ for the shaded region.

42. The answer is B.

The equation $F = Kx$ is linear in x with slope K

43. The answer is B.

Mr. A's average speed is equal to 8 miles per hour.
Let us compute the time Mr. B would take to complete the 100 miles. He will complete the first two miles in 2/10 = 1/5 hours. The next mile in 1/7 hours. So, he completes the first three miles in 1/5 + 1/7 = 12/32 hours. He would complete the first 99 miles in 33*12/32 hours. The 100th mile would be completed in ½*1/5 hours = 1/10 hours. So total time taken = 33*12/32 + 1/10 = 12.0475
Hence, average speed for Mr. B = 100/12.475 = 8.016 miles per hour

44. The answer is D.

Area of circle = πr^2 where r is the radius of the circle. To double this expression is to double r^2. This is same as scaling r by $\sqrt{2}$. Now, $\sqrt{2} = 1.414..$ Hence, r should be increased by about 41.4%

45. The answer is C.

The peak of the graph in that week lies on the Friday of that week.

46. The answer is C.

Tuesday has the lowest price for both weeks.

47. The answer is C.

There are 34 students in the class. The median is the mean of the ages of the 17th and 18th oldest students i.e. $\frac{12+13}{2} = 12.5$

48. The answer is D.

Depending on the age of the student joining, the median may increase or decrease.

49. The answer is B.

For a right triangle the hypotenuse is the longest side. If the none of the given sides is the hypotenuse, then the hypotenuse would have length $\sqrt{3^2 + 4^2} = \sqrt{25} = 5$. However, this is not one of the choices available. The side of length 4 units could be the hypotenuse. Then the other side would have length $\sqrt{4^2 - 3^2} = \sqrt{7}$

50. The answer is D.

Let Lulu's initial speed be $x\ miles\ per\ hour$.

The speed on the second day would be $x + 10\%\ of\ x = 1.1 * x$.

The speed on the third day would be $1.1 * 1.1x = 1.21x$.

The speed decreases on the fourth day by 10%. Hence, speed on fourth day = 90% of third day's

speed = $0.9 * 1.21x = 1.089x$

Speed on the final day = $0.9 * 1.089x = 0.9801x$

Average speed over the four days = $\frac{x+1.1x+1.21x+1.089x+0.9801x}{4} = \frac{5.3791x}{4} = 1.344775x$

Since she maintains an average speed of 50 miles per hour: $1.344775x = 50$

Therefore, $x = 37.18$ miles per hour

51. The answer is: 69.5

The sum of the weights of the original group of 9 kids = $9 * 70 = 630$
When one more kid is added, the new sum $= 630 + 65 = 695$
New mean = $\frac{695}{10} = 69.5$

52. The answer is: 11

If n denotes the number of quarters in Skyler's pocket, the number of dimes would be (n+4).
Since he has a total of $4.45 in his pocket we can write the equation

$$0.25n + 0.10(n + 4) = 4.25$$

Solving, we get n = 11

53. The answer is: $-\frac{4}{3}$

Expanding,

$$(1+3i)(c+4i) = (c-12) + (3c+4)i$$

For this to be real, $3c+4$ should be 0 i.e. $c = -\frac{4}{3}$

54. The answer is: 2

$(1.5, 8)$ and $(1,7)$ are points on the line $Slope = \frac{8-7}{1.5-1} = \frac{1}{0.5} = 2$

55. The answer is: 20

Green apples account for $\frac{1}{2} * \frac{20}{100} = \frac{1}{10}$ of all fruits in the basket. Since the number of green apples is 2, the total number of fruits in the basket should be 20.

56. The answer is ±2

$x^2 - 4x + 3$ is the quadratic equations whose roots sum up to 4 and have product 3. Solving this quadratic equation we get the roots as 3 and 1. Hence, the difference is either 2 or -2.

57. The answer is: $\frac{2}{3}$

Denote the density of wood by d_{wood} and that of water by d_{water}. The weight of the bock of wood is $30 * d_{wood} * g$ where g is the acceleration due to gravity. The weight of water displaced is $20 * d_{water} * g$.

By Archimedes' principle, we have

$$30 * d_{wood} * g = 20 * d_{water} * g$$

This gives, $\frac{d_{wood}}{d_{water}} = \frac{2}{3}$

58. The answer is: 8

Note the series $2^1 = 2, 2^2 = 4, 2^3 = 8, 2^4 = 16, 2^5 = 32, 2^6 = 64, 2^7 = 128, \ldots$. The last digit is either 2, 4, 8 or 6 depending on whether the exponent, on division by 4, has remainder 1, 2, 3 or 4. 375 on division by 4 has remainder 3, hence the last digit should be 8.

TEST 5

1. The answer is D.

$$x - 5 = k \land k = -2$$
$$x - 5 = -2$$
$$x = 5 - 2$$
$$x = 3$$

$$5x + 2 = 5 \times 3 + 2 = 15 + 2 = 17$$

2. The answer is A.

$$(3 - 4i) - (1 + 7i) = 3 - 4i - 1 - 7i = 2 - 11i$$

3. The answer is A.

From Monday to Friday the grocery store is opened t hours every day. The total number of hours the grocery store is opened on these 5 days is $5t$. On Saturday the grocery store is opened k hours, and on Sunday is closed. Therefore, the total number of hours the grocery store is opened during the week is $5t + k$.

4. The answer is D.

For t items sold this month Noah earned $t \times \$n = nt$ dollars. Since his fixed salary is $\$m$, Noah's total earnings this month is $m + nt$.

5. The answer is B.

$$(4x^2 - 3x + 6) - (-2x^2 + 5x - 3) = 4x^2 - 3x + 6 + 2x^2 - 5x + 3 =$$
$$= 6x^2 - 8x + 9$$

6. The answer is A.

w – Emma's weight after m months
m – number of months
2 – Emma's decrease in weight per month
96 – Emma's initial weight

7. The answer is C.

$$F = \frac{GMm}{r^2}$$
$$Fr^2 = GMm$$
$$m = \frac{Fr^2}{GM}$$

8. The answer is B.

$$a - 2b = -4$$
$$a = 2b - 4$$

$$\frac{a+2}{a+2b} = \frac{2b-4+2}{2b-4+2b} = \frac{2b-2}{4b-4} = \frac{2(b-1)}{4(b-1)} = \frac{2}{4} = \frac{1}{2}$$

9. The answer is A.

$$x + y = -4$$
$$x - y = 6$$

Add equations.

$$x + y + x - y = -4 + 6$$
$$2x = 2$$
$$x = \frac{2}{2} = 1$$

$$x + y = -4$$
$$1 + y = -4$$
$$y = -4 - 1 = -5$$

10. The answer is B.

$$f(2) = 4 \Leftrightarrow 4 = 3 \times 2 - a \Leftrightarrow 4 - 6 = -a \Leftrightarrow -2 = -a \Leftrightarrow a = 2$$
$$f(-2) = 3(-2) - 2 = -6 - 2 = -8$$

11. The answer is A.

$$h = 25.5 + 3.5t$$
$$50 = 25.5 + 3.5t$$
$$10 \times 50 = 10 \times 25.5 + 10 \times 3.5t$$
$$500 = 255 + 35t$$
$$500 - 255 = 35t$$
$$245 = 35t$$
$$t = \frac{245}{35} = 7$$

12. The answer is C.

All points on the line parallel to the x-axis have the same y-coordinate. Since the line passes through the point (2,3), all points on that line have y-coordinate equal to 3. Therefore, the point (-1,3) lies on the line.

13. The answer is A.

$$\frac{1}{x}-\frac{1}{x-1}=\frac{1(x-1)}{x(x-1)}-\frac{1x}{x(x-1)}=\frac{x-1-x}{x(x-1)}=\frac{-1}{x(x-1)}=\frac{1}{-x(x-1)}=$$
$$=\frac{1}{x(1-x)}$$

14. The answer is D.

$$2^x2^y=2^{x+y}=2^3=8$$

15. The answer is C.

$$(ax+4)(2x+5)=6x^2+bx+20$$
$$2ax^2+5ax+8x+20=6x^2+bx+20$$
$$2ax^2+(5a+8)x+20=6x^2+bx+20$$

$$2a=6$$
$$a=3$$

$$5a+8=b$$
$$5\times 3+8=b$$
$$23=b$$

16. The answer is: -4

$$p^2-16=0$$
$$p^2=16$$
$$p=\pm\sqrt{16}=\pm 4$$

$$p<0\Rightarrow p=-4$$

17. The answer is: 1.4

$$\measuredangle BCA=\measuredangle ADC=90^o$$
$$\measuredangle CAB=\measuredangle CAD$$
$$\Delta ABC\sim\Delta ADC$$

$$AB:AC=BC:x$$

$AB^2 = BC^2 + AC^2 = 4^2 + 3^2 = 16 + 9 = 25$
$AB = \sqrt{25} = 5$

$5:3 = 4:x$
$5x = 3 \times 4$
$x = \frac{12}{5} = 1.4$

18. The answer is: -2

$x - 2y = -4$
$x + 3y = 1$

$3x - 6y = -12$
$2x + 6y = 2$

$3x - 6y + 2x + 6y = -12 + 2$
$5x = -10$
$x = -2$

19. The answer is: $\frac{4}{5}$

$\sin^2 x + \cos^2 x = 1$
$\cos^2 x = 1 - \sin^2 x = 1 - \left(\frac{3}{5}\right)^2 = 1 - \frac{9}{25} = \frac{25}{25} - \frac{9}{25} = \frac{16}{25}$
$\cos x = \sqrt{\frac{16}{25}} = \frac{4}{5}$

20. The answer is: 0

$\sqrt{12} - \sqrt{75} + \sqrt{27} = \sqrt{4 \times 3} - \sqrt{25 \times 3} + \sqrt{9 \times 3} = 2\sqrt{3} - 5\sqrt{3} + 3\sqrt{3} = 0$

21. The answer is B.

Horizontal line represents the constant speed of the bus. Between 4th and 8th minute the bus travels at the constant speed. Therefore, it is 4 minutes.

22. The answer is D.

The equation of line which passes through the origin is $y = kx$. Since point (3,-5) lies on that line we have

$-5 = k \times 3 \Rightarrow k = -\frac{5}{3}$

Since point (-6,y) also lies on that line we have

$y = -\frac{5}{3} \times (-6) = 5 \times 2 = 10$

23. The answer is C.

$\sphericalangle CDE + 30^o + 75^o = 180^o$
$\sphericalangle CDE = 180^o - 30^o - 75^o = 75^o$
$x^o = \sphericalangle CDE = 75^o$

24. The answer is B.

$4x - 5 + 9 = 12$
$4x + 4 = 12$
$4x = 8$
$x = 2$
$2x = 2 \times 2 = 4$

25. The answer is A.

A graph with a positive association between *x* and *y* would have the points on the graph closely aligned with a line that has a positive slope. Of the four graphs, the points on graph A are most closely aligned with a line with a positive slope.

26. The answer is C.

$3\ yards = (3 \times 3)\ feet = 9\ feet = (9 \times 12) inches = 108\ inches$

$\{Number\ of\ tiles\ in\ a\ row\} = \frac{\{Length\ of\ the\ floor\}}{\{Length\ of\ the\ tile\}} = \frac{108\ inches}{4\ inches} = 27$

27. The answer is C.

Minimum number of citizens on the graph is 3.

$\frac{30{,}000}{3} = 10{,}000$

Therefore, an appropriate label for the vertical axis of the graph is ten thousands.

28. The answer is A.

All positive values less than 4 are solutions. Since absolute value is always positive, then all negative values greater than -4 are solutions. Zero is also a solution. So, all numbers between -4 and 4 are solutions.

29. The answer is B.

$$v = 40 + 4a$$
$$-4a = 40 - v$$
$$4a = v - 40$$
$$a = \frac{v - 40}{4}$$

30. The answer is C.

$$v = 40 + 4a$$
$$50 = 40 + 4a$$
$$-4a = 40 - 50$$
$$-4a = -10$$
$$a = \frac{-10}{-4} = 2.5$$

31. The answer is D.

$$3x - 5 > 6 - 2x$$
$$3x + 2x > 6 + 5$$
$$5x > 11$$
$$x > \frac{11}{5}$$
$$x > 2\frac{1}{5}$$

32. The answer is C.

The following numbers appear in the graph: 5, 2, 3, 5, 3, 5, 7

Number	2	3	5	7
Frequency	1	2	3	1

Mode is the most frequent value. Therefore, it is 5.

33. The answer is B.

$$\frac{\{Number\ of\ female\ cats\}}{\{Total\ number\ of\ pets\}} \times 100\% = \frac{18}{80} \times 100\% = 22.5\%$$

34. The answer is C.

The range is the difference between maximum and minimum value.
$\{max\ value\} = 45$

$\{min\ value\} = 5$
$range = \{max\ value\} - \{min\ value\} = 45 - 5 = 40$

35. The answer is C.

The initial level of gas in the tank is the *l*-intercept of line. Therefore, it is 50.

36. The answer is D.

It is the y-coordinate of the point on the line which x-coordinate is 300. According to graph, it is 32.

37. The answer is D.

The maximum point is the highest point. According to graph, its coordinates are (-2,4). Therefore, the y-coordinate of the maximum point is 4.

38. Then answer is C.

Substitue the coordinates of points to check whether they satisfy both inequalities.
$(-1,-3) \Rightarrow x = -1, y = 3$
$y > x - 3$
$3 > -1 - 3$
$3 > -4$ T
$y < 4x + 3$
$3 < 4(-1) + 3$
$3 < -4 + 3$
$3 < -1 \perp$

Therefore, point (-1,3) is not the solution of the system of inequalities, because it doesn't satisfy the second inequality.

39. The answer is D.

g – number of girls
b – number of boys
There are 245 boys and girls in the cinema: $b + g = 245$
There are 23 more girls than boys: $g - b = 23$
$b + g + g - b = 245 + 23$
$2g = 268$
$g = \frac{268}{2} = 134$

40. The answer is C.

Sarah weighed $57 + 3 = 60$ kg before she lost 3 kg.

$$\frac{3\ kg}{60\ kg} \times 100\% = 5\%$$

41. The answer is A.

Years of experience of employees

	Less than 10	Between 10 and 20	Between 20 and 30	More than 30	Total
Males	12	14	8	6	40
Females	6	24	16	4	50
Total	18	38	24	10	90

There are 18 employees with less than 10 years of experience. We choose at random from 90 employees.

$$\frac{18}{90} = \frac{1}{5}$$

42. The answer is A.

Number of students at Faculty of Natural Sciences and Mathematics

Department	Year			
	2010	2011	2012	2013
Math	120	90	110	86
Physics	86	90	96	108
Biology	94	76	88	92
Chemistry	108	120	115	103

The maximum number of students at the Math Department was 120 in 2010.

43. The answer is C.

Number of students at Faculty of Natural Sciences and Mathematics

Department	Year			
	2010	2011	2012	2013
Math	120	90	110	86
Physics	86	90	96	108
Biology	94	76	88	92
Chemistry	108	120	115	103

The minimum number of students was 76, in 2011, at the Department of Biology.

44. The answer is A.

The equation of the circle is $(x-p)^2+(y-q)^2=r^2$, where the center of the circle is $C(p,q)$ and radius is r.

$C(2,-2) \Rightarrow p=2, q=-2, r=2$

$(x-p)^2+(y-q)^2=r^2$

$(x-2)^2+\left(y-(-2)\right)^2=2^2$

$(x-2)^2+(y+2)^2=4$

45. The answer is C.

$t=4$

$P=\frac{1}{4}t^2+t-5=\frac{1}{4}\times 4^2+4-5=\frac{1}{4}\times 16-1=4-1=3$

Since P is given in millions of dollars, the profit is $3,000,000.

46. The answer is D.

The number of girls in the class is $12.5\% \times 32=\frac{12.5}{100}\times 32=4$

Therefore, there are $32-4=28$ boys.

47. The answer is C.

$$\frac{\{Polled\ students\ who\ love\ math\}}{\{Polled\ students\}}=\frac{\{All\ students\ in\ school\ who\ love\ math\}}{\{All\ students\ in\ school\}}$$

$8:30=x:540$

$30x=8\times 540$

$x=\frac{8\times 540}{30}=\frac{8\times 54}{3}=8\times 18=144$

48. The answer is C.

Draw a graph of a line $2x+3y-12=0$.

x	0	6
y	4	0

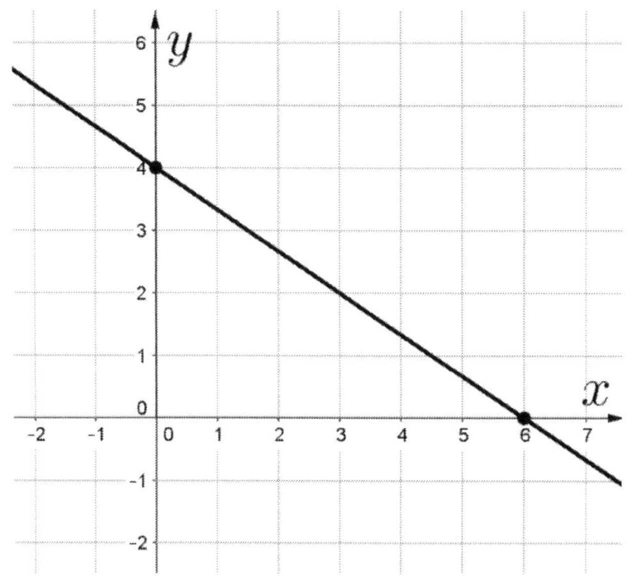

Therefore, line doesn't pass through the III quadrant.

49. The answer is D.

If $p(x)$ is a polynomial, $a \in R$ and $p(a) = 0$, then $p(x)$ is divisible by $(x - a)$. Since $p(-1) = 0$, follows that $p(x)$ is divisible by $\left(x - (-1)\right) = x + 1$. Therefore, $x + 1$ is a factor of $p(x)$.

50. The answer is C.

$$ax^2 + bx + c = a(x - x_1) + (x - x_2)$$

$$x^2 - 6x - 16 = 0$$

$$a = 1, b = -6, c = -16$$

$$x_{1,2} = \frac{-b \pm \sqrt{b^2 - 4ac}}{2a} = \frac{-(-6) \pm \sqrt{(-6)^2 - 4 \times 1 \times (-16)}}{2 \times 1} = \frac{6 \pm \sqrt{36 + 64}}{2} =$$

$$= \frac{6 \pm \sqrt{100}}{2} = \frac{6 \pm 10}{2}$$

$$x_1 = \frac{6 + 10}{2} = \frac{16}{2} = 8$$

$$x_2 = \frac{6 - 10}{2} = \frac{-4}{2} = -2$$

$$x^2 - 6x - 16 = 1(x - 8)\left(x - (-2)\right) = (x - 8)(x + 2)$$

$$y = (x - 8)(x + 2)$$

51. The answers can be: -9, -8, -7, -6 or -5

$1 < y < 5$
$-1 > -y > -5$
$-5 < -y < -1$
$-5 < x < -3$
$-5 - 5 < -y + x < -1 - 3$
$-10 < x - y < -4$

Any number between -10 and -4 is a solution.

52. The answer is: 5

x – number of months
$68 - 3x < 55$
$68 - 55 < 3x$
$13 < 3x$
$3x > 13$
$x > \frac{13}{3}$
$x > 4\frac{1}{3}$

Olivia will weigh less than 55 kg after 5 months.

53. The answer is: 4

The number of employees was less than 40 in 2010, 2011, 2012 and 2013. It is 4 years.

54. The answer is: 10

$1\ km = 1{,}000\ m$
$1\ h = 60\ min$
$1\ min = 60\ sec$
$1\ h = 60\ min = (60 \times 60)\ sec = 3{,}600\ sec$
$$36\frac{km}{h} = 36 \times \frac{1{,}000\ m}{3{,}600\ s} = \frac{1{,}000\ m}{\frac{3{,}600\ s}{36}} = \frac{1{,}000\ m}{100\ s} = 10\frac{m}{s}$$

55. The answer is: 10

$d = 12$
$2r = 12$
$r = 6$

$V = r^2\pi h$

$$h = \frac{V}{r^2\pi} = \frac{360\pi}{6^2\pi} = \frac{360}{36} = 10$$

56. The answer is: 3

The intersection point has coordinates $(x, 0)$.

$$y = \frac{x^2 - 6x + 9}{x + 4}$$
$$0 = \frac{x^2 - 6x + 9}{x + 4}$$
$$0(x + 4) = (x + 4)\frac{x^2 - 6x + 9}{x + 4}$$
$$0 = x^2 - 6x + 9$$
$$0 = (x - 3)^2$$
$$0 = x - 3$$
$$x = 3$$

57. The answer is: 0.94

Since the number of employees falls, the rate is negative.

$$p = -6\%$$
$$x = 1 + \frac{p}{100} = 1 + \frac{-6}{100} = 1 - 0.06 = 0.94$$

58. The answer is: 1,600

$$t = 5$$
$$2{,}200 \times (0.94)^5 \approx 1{,}615 \approx 1600$$

TEST 6

1. The answer is A.

   To eliminate fractions, both sides of the first equation are multiplied by 27(x + y) giving:

   $27(x + y)\left(\frac{1}{x+y}\right) = 27(x + y)\left(\frac{4}{27}\right)$

   27(1) = 4(x + y)

   27 = 4x + 4y *(equation 3)*

   Expanding the second equation:

   33 = 4(2x − y)
   33 = 8x − 4y *(equation 4)*

   Adding equation 3 and equation 4 gives:

   60 = 12x

   $x = \frac{60}{12}$

   x = 5

2. The answer is D.

   Simplifying the equations, we have:

   Equation 1: 4k – 5 = 2(2k – 3) + 1
   4k – 5 = 4k – 6 + 1
   -5 = -5 (Identity equation)
   Equation 2: 2(b - 4) = 2b – 7
   2b – 8 = 2b – 7
   -8 = -7 (Contradiction equation)
   Equation 3: 3x + 7 = 2x – 5
   3x - 2x + 7 = 2x – 2x – 5
   x = -12 (Conditional equation)

3. The answer is B.

   Let x be the smallest integer. Thus, the four consecutive integers would be x, x+1, x+2, and x+3. Since we are told that thirty times the largest of the four consecutive integers is fifty-six more than seven times the sum of the four consecutive integers, then we have

   30(x+3) = 7[x + (x+1)+ (x+2)+(x+3)] + 56
   30x + 90 = 7(4x+6) + 56
   30x + 90 = 28x + 98
   2x = 8
   x = 4

Therefore, the largest integer would be x + 3 = 4 + 3 = 7.

4. The answer is A.

   Let x represent the number of regular priced tickets sold, and 300 – x is the number of discounted tickets sold. Then we have

   $$8x + 6(300 - x) = 2{,}040$$
   $$8x + 1{,}800 - 6x = 2{,}040$$
   $$2x + 1{,}800 = 2{,}040$$
   $$2x = 240$$
   $$x = 120 \text{ regular priced tickets}$$

5. The answer is A.

   The roots of the curve in the graph are all the values of x for which y = 0. Based on the graph of the curve, the roots are -2, 2 and 4.

   Hence, the sum of all the roots are -2 + 2 + 4 = 4.

6. The answer is A.

   The problem is about maximizing the contribution margin from the scarce resources-labor hours. The problem can be solved by translating it into equations:

   Let x = ordinary and y = folding:
   Assembly Department (constraint: 200 hours available): 2x+ 2y = 200
   Sewing Department (constraint: 180 hours available): 2x + y = 180

   Next is to get the intersection of the two equations. Solving for the values of x and y by elimination, we get

   $$(2x + 2y = 200) - (2x + y = 180) = (y=20)$$

   Since y = 20, then 2x + 2y = 200 → 2x + 2(20) = 200 → 2x + 40 = 200 → x = 80.

   The best product combination therefore is 80 units of ordinary and 20 units of folding. The maximum possible profit for this product combination would be

   $$\$20(80) + \$30(20) = \$2{,}200.00$$

7. The answer is D.

   i. False

   $$f(x) = x^3 - 10x^2 + 33x - 36 \text{ factor by grouping method}$$

$f(x) = (x - 3)(x^2 - 7x + 12)$
$0 = (x-3)(x-4)(x-3)$
$x = 3, 4, 3$
Largest Possible Factor = 4

ii. False
Any quadratic equation will have real and distinct roots if the discriminant $D > 0$
The discriminant D of a quadratic equation $ax^2 + bx + c = 0$ is given by $b^2 - 4ac$
In this question, the value of $D = 36 - 4k$
If $D > 0$, then $36 > 4k$ or $k < 9$.
Therefore, the highest integral value that k can take is 8.

iii. False
Express 72 as a product of its prime factors, $72 = 2^3 \times 3^2$
Number of factors of 72 is $(3 + 1) \times (2 + 1) = 12$
Hence, it can be expressed as a product of two positive integers in 6 ways. For each such combination, we can have a combination in which both the factors could be negative. Therefore, 6 more combinations - taking it to total of 12 combinations.

8. The answer is C.

Substituting $x = 1$ and $y = -2$ into $y = mx + c$ gives:
$$-2 = m + c \quad \text{(Equation 1)}$$
Substituting $x = 3\frac{1}{2}$ and $y=10\frac{1}{2}$ into $y = mx + c$ gives:
$$10\frac{1}{2} = 3\frac{1}{2}m + c \quad \text{(Equation 2)}$$

Subtracting equation (1) from equation (2) gives $12\frac{1}{2} = 2\frac{1}{2}$ m from which $m = 5$.
Substituting $m = 5$ into equation (1) gives: $-2 = 5 + c$
Therefore, $c = -2 - 5 = -7$

9. The answer is A.

For a simultaneous solution the values of y must be equal, hence the right hand side of each equation is equated. Thus $5x - 4 - 2x^2 = 6x - 7$
Rearranging gives $5x - 4 - 2x^2 - 6x + 7 = 0 \rightarrow -x + 3 - 2x^2 = 0$ or $2x^2 + x - 3 = 0$
Factoring gives $(2x + 3)(x - 1) = 0$ or $x = -\frac{3}{2}$ or $x = 1$

In the equation $y = 6x - 7$, when $x = -\frac{3}{2}$, $y = 6(-\frac{3}{2}) - 7 = -16$ and when $x = 1$, $y = 6 - 7 = -1$.

Hence the simultaneous solutions are $x = -\frac{3}{2}$, $y=-16$ and $x = 1$, $y = -1$. Therefore, the difference of highest value of x and lowest value of y is $1- (-1) = 2$.

10. The answer is C.

Statement 1: False

$5x + 7 < 3(x + 1)$

$5x + 7 < 3x + 3$

$2x + 7 < 3$

$2x < -4$

$x < -2$

Statement 2: False

$3(x - 2) + 4 > 2(2x - 3)$

$3x - 6 + 4 > 4x - 6$

$3x - 2 > 4x - 6$

$-2 > x - 6$

$4 > x$

$x < 4$

Statement 3: Correct

$2x - 5 + 5 < 1$

$2x < 6$

$x < 3$

11. The answer is A.

Any quadratic equation will have real and distinct roots if the discriminant is greater than 0. The discriminant of a quadratic equation of the form $ax^2 + bx + c = 0$ is given by $b^2 - 4ac$. In this question, the value of the discriminant is $36 - 4k$. If the discriminant is greater than 0, then $36 - 4k > 0 \rightarrow 36 > 4k$ or $k < 9$. Therefore, the highest integral value that k can take is 8.

12. The answer is A.

Substitute y in the equation of the circle by $(-x - \frac{1}{2})$ as follows

$(x - 2)^2 + (-x - \frac{1}{2} + 3)^2 = 4$

$(x^2 - 4x + 4) + (x^2 - 5x + \frac{25}{4}) = 4$

$2x^2 - 9x + \frac{25}{4} = 0$

Solving for x, we have $x = \frac{9+\sqrt{31}}{4}$ and $x = \frac{9-\sqrt{31}}{4}$.

Substitute the values of x already obtained into the equation $y = -x - \frac{1}{2}$ to obtain the values for y as follows y = $\frac{-11-\sqrt{31}}{4}$ and y = $\frac{-11+\sqrt{31}}{4}$.

The two points of intersection of the two equations are given by;

$(\frac{9+\sqrt{31}}{4}, \frac{-11-\sqrt{31}}{4})$ and $(\frac{9-\sqrt{31}}{4}, \frac{-11+\sqrt{31}}{4})$. This is approximately (3.64, -4.14) and (0.86, -1.36).

13. The answer is A.

If the roots of a quadratic equation are α and β then (x – α)(x – β) = 0.
Hence, if $\alpha = \frac{1}{3}$ and β = −2, then

$(x - \frac{1}{3})(x - (-2)) = 0$

$x^2 - \frac{x}{3} + 2x - \frac{2}{3} = 0$

$x^2 + \frac{5}{3}x - \frac{2}{3} = 0$

Hence $3x^2 + 5x - 2 = 0$

14. The answer is D.

Let x be the number. Then,

$4 + 10(\frac{1}{x}) = \frac{22}{x}$

$\frac{10}{x} - \frac{22}{x} = -4$

$-\frac{12}{x} = -4$

-4x = -12

x = 3

15. The answer is C.

Multiplying by $\frac{3+\sqrt{8}}{3+\sqrt{8}}$, we get $3 - \sqrt{8} \times \frac{3+\sqrt{8}}{3+\sqrt{(8)}} = \frac{(3-\sqrt{8})(3+\sqrt{8})}{3+\sqrt{8}} = \frac{3^2-(\sqrt{8})^2}{3+\sqrt{8}} = \frac{9-8}{3+\sqrt{8}} = \frac{1}{3+\sqrt{8}}$.

16. The answer is: 18

We are given that $\sqrt{X+Y} = 6$. Squaring both sides of the equation, we get $X + Y = 36$.

Since $\sqrt{X} - \sqrt{Y} = 0$, then $\sqrt{X} = \sqrt{Y}$. Squaring both sides of the equation, we get $X = Y$.

Replacing this in the first equation, we get $X + Y = X + X = 2X = 36$ or $X = 18$.

17. The answer is: 1 or -2

Squaring both sides, we get
$(3x+1)^2 = \left(\sqrt{3x^2+13}\right)^2$
$9x^2 + 6x + 1 = 3x^2 + 13$
$6x^2 + 6x - 12 = 0$
$x^2 + x - 2 = 0.$

Solving for x, we get $x = 1$ or $x = -2$.

18. The answer is: 3

The radius of the poké ball is 2.5 centimeters (since the diameter has to be 5 cm). Each colored section of the circle is 1/6 of the whole circle.

The sector area formula: $\left(\frac{1}{6}\right)\pi r^2$
$= \left(\frac{1}{6}\right)\pi(2.5)^2$
$= 3.27\ cm^2$

Therefore, we can round it off to 3 cm^2

19. The answer is: 20

4 scooters x 5 options = 20 types of scooters

20. The answer is: 60

$\frac{\pi}{3} * \frac{180}{\pi} = 60°$

21. The answer is B.

Let b be the number of runs scored by byes, w be the number of runs scored by wides and r be the number of runs scored by runs. We are given that w + b + r = 232.

The runs scored by the two best players are 26 times the wides. This means r = 26w.

There are 8 more byes than wides. This means b = w + 8.

Thus, our equation becomes w + b + r = w + (w+8) + 26w = 232. This gives us w = 8, r = 208 and b = 16.

The ratio of the runs scored by George and Michael is 6x:7x, for some integer x.This means 6x + 7x = 13x = 208, or x = 16.

Therefore, the number of runs scored by George is 6x = 6*16 = 96.

22. The answer is A.

The maximum/minimum temperatures for brewing Earl Grey tea can be represented by $|x - 210| = 5$.

Maximum Temperature:

x – 210 = 5
x = 215°

Minimum Temperature:

x – 210 = -5
x = 205°

23. The answer is C.

Given that $\frac{x-y}{z} = 1$, this means $z \neq 0$. Thus, we can write $\frac{x-y}{z} = 1$ as $x - y = z$.

Since $x = 1$,then $x - y = z$ can be written as $1 - y = z$. If $z = 0$, then $1 - y = 0$ or $y = 1$. However, since $z \neq 0$, then it follows that $y \neq 1$.

24. The answer is B.

So, the term 'decile' is probably new to you. It's a statistical measure similar to the 'quartile'. While the quartile sorts data into four parts, the decile sorts data into ten parts. The data has to be ordered and you have to break it up into ten equal parts (or groups). In this question, we are given 20 numbers. After ordering them, we can simply group them in pairs to get 10 groups.

7	14	15	17	17	19	20	21	21	22
22	23	24	26	27	28	29	30	32	37

The first decile group is obtained by splitting the ranked set into 10 equal groups and selecting the first group, i.e. the numbers 7 and 14. The second decile group are the numbers 15 and 17, and so on.

Thus, the 8th decile group contains the numbers 27 and 28

25. The correct answer is D.

The probability of selecting a microchip within the required tolerance standard is $\frac{73}{100}$. The first microchip drawn is now replaced and a second one is drawn from the batch of 100. The probability of this capacitor being within the required tolerance standard is also $\frac{73}{100}$. Thus, the probability of selecting a microchip within the required tolerance standard for both the first and the second draw is: $\frac{73}{100} \times \frac{73}{100} = \frac{5,329}{10,000}$ or 53.29 %

26. The correct answer is C.

Let p be the probability that a lightbulb will not pass quality control, that is, defective, and let q be the probability that a lightbulb will pass quality control, that is, satisfactory.

Then, p = 5% and q = 95%. The sample number is 7.

The probabilities of drawing 0, 1, 2, ..., n defective lightbulbs are given by the successive terms of the expansion of (q+p)n, taken from left to right.

In this problem (q + p)n = (0.95 + 0.05)7 = 0.957 + 7 × 0.956 × 0.05 +21 × 0.955 × 0.052 + . . .

Thus the probability of no defective lightbulb is:

0.957 = 0.6983

The probability of 1 defective lightbulb is:

7 × 0.956 × 0.05 = 0.2573

The probability of 2 defective lightbulbs is:

21 × 0.955 × 0.052 = 0.0406, and so on.

To determine the probability that more than two lightbulbs are defective, the sum of the probabilities of 3 lightbulbs, 4 lightbulbs, 5 lightbulbs, 6 lightbulbs and 7 lightbulbs being defective can be determined. An easier way to find this sum is to find 1−(sum of 0 lightbulb, 1 lightbulb and 2 lightbulbs being defective), since the sum of all the terms is unity. Thus, the probability of there being more than two lightbulbs will not pass quality control is 1 − (0.6983 + 0.2573 + 0.0406), that is, 0.0038 or 0.38 %

27. The answer is B.

Number of ways = ${}_nC_r = {}_{16}C_{11}$

$= \frac{16!}{11!(16-11)!}$

$= \frac{16 \times 15 \times 14 \times 13 \times 12 \times 11!}{11!5!}$

= 4,368

28. The answer is A.

The volume of the stone block is 330 cubic yards, and the dimensions will be x yards high by (13x-11) yards long and (13x-15) yards wide.

Since volume = height × width × length, we have

$$330 = x(13x - 11)(13x - 15)$$
$$330 = 169x^3 - 338x^2 + 165x$$
$$169x^3 - 338x^2 + 165x - 330 = 0$$
$$169x^2(x - 2) + 165(x - 2) = 0$$
$$(169x^2 + 165)(x - 2) = 0$$

The only real solution is x = 2, so 13x -11 = 15 and 13x -15 = 11. The block is 2 yards high. The dimensions are 2 yards by 15 yards by 11 yards.

29. The answer is B.

$e^x = 1 + x + \frac{x^2}{2!} + \frac{x^3}{3!} + \frac{x^4}{4!} + \ldots$

Hence $e^{0.5} = 1 + 0.5 + \frac{0.5^2}{2!} + \frac{0.5^3}{3!} + \frac{0.5^4}{4!} + \frac{0.5^5}{5!} + \frac{0.5^6}{6!} = 1 + 0.5 + 0.125 + 0.020833 + 0.0026042 +$ $0.0002604 + 0.0000217$, that is, $e^{0.5} = 1.64872$ correct to 6 significant figures.

Hence $5e^{0.5} = 5(1.64872) = 8.2436$, correct to 5 significant figures

30. The answer is D.

$r = (\frac{A}{P})^{1/t} - 1$ where A = \$11,220.41, P = \$8,000, t = 5

$r = (\frac{11{,}220.41}{8{,}000})^{0.2} - 1 = (1.4)^{0.2} - 1 = 1.07 - 1 = 0.07$

r = 7.0%

31. The answer is D.

The function is written in the form $y = ax^2 + bx + c$ where a = -16, b=60, and c= 0. Because a is negative, the parabola opens downward. Therefore, the maximum height of the ball occurs at the vertex of the parabola.

The x coordinate of the vertex is given by

$$x = \frac{-b}{2a} = \frac{-60}{2(-16)} = \frac{-60}{-32} = \frac{15}{8}$$

Substituting x= $\frac{15}{8}$ into the question, we have

$y = -16(\frac{15}{8})^2 + 60(\frac{15}{8})$

$y = \frac{225}{4}$

The vertex is $(\frac{15}{8}, \frac{225}{4})$ or (1.875, 56.25).

The ball reaches its maximum height of 56.25 feet after 1.875 seconds.

32. The answer is C.

From the formula, substitute the values

$$f\,(x,y) = 36{,}000 + 40x + 30y + \frac{xy}{100}$$

$$f\,(2{,}000, 5{,}000) = 36{,}000 + 40(2{,}000) + 30(5{,}000) + \frac{(2{,}000)(5{,}000)}{100} = \$366{,}000$$

33. The answer is C.

If the major axis = 15.0 centimeters, then the semi-major axis = 7.5 centimeters.
If the minor axis = 9.0 centimeters, then the semi-minor axis = 4.5 centimeters

Area = πab = π(7.5)(4.5) = 106.0 centimeters^2

34. The answer is A.

Radius of cylindrical head = 0.5 cm and length of cylindrical head = 2 mm = 0.2 cm
Hence, volume of cylindrical head = $\pi r^2 h = \pi(0.5)^2(0.2) = 0.1571$ cm^3

Radius of cylindrical shaft = 1 mm = 0.1 cm and length of cylindrical shaft = 1.5 cm
Volume of cylindrical shaft = $\pi r^2 h = \pi(0.1)^2(1.5) = 0.0471$ cm^3

Total volume of 1 metal bolt = 0.1571 + 0.0471 = 0.2042 cm^3
Volume of metal in 2,000 metal bolts = 2,000 × 0.2042 = 408.4 cm^3

35. The answer is C.

Jordan can run R miles in H hours, and bike B miles in three times the same number of hours, or 3H. Therefore, the combined distance that Jordan can travel in the combined hours would be $R + B$ miles in $H + 3H = 4H$ hours. Since average speed is given to be $\frac{distance}{time}$, then Jordan's average speed is $\frac{R+B}{4H}$ miles per hour.

36. The answer is B.

When $a = 0$, then $(a - 1) \times b = (-1) \times b = -b$.
When $b = 0$, then $(a - 1) \times 0 = 0$.

37. The answer is B.

Let A be Andrea's age now and S be Sally's age now. Three years ago, Andrea's age was four times of Sally's age.

This can be written as $A - 3 = 4 \times (S - 3)$.

Four years from now, Andrea's age will be three times Sally's age.

This can be written as $A + 4 = 3 \times (S + 4)$. We have two distinct linear equations with two unknowns. Solving for the values of A and S:

$A - 3 = 4S - 12$ (Eq. 1) and $A + 4 = 3S + 12$ (Eq. 2)

Subtracting Eq. 2 from Eq. 1, we get $-7 = S - 24$ or $S = 17$.

This means $A - 3 = 4(17) - 12 \rightarrow A - 3 = 56$ or $A = 59$.

Therefore, $A - S = 59 - 17 = 42$.

38. The answer is A.

There are several ways to solve for the solution of the system of linear equations. One way is by substitution.

Since $2x - 3y = -1$, solving for x in terms of y and we get $x = \frac{3y-1}{2}$

Replacing this value of x in the other equation, we get
$3\left(\frac{3y-1}{2}\right) + 5y = \frac{1}{2} \rightarrow \frac{9y-3}{2} + 5y = \frac{1}{2} \rightarrow \frac{9y-3}{2} + \frac{10y}{2} = \frac{1}{2}$

$\rightarrow 9y - 3 + 10y = 1 \rightarrow 19y = 4 \rightarrow y = \frac{4}{19}$.

This means $x = \frac{3y-1}{2} = \frac{3\times\left(\frac{4}{19}\right)-1}{2} = \frac{\left(\frac{12}{19}\right)-1}{2} = -\frac{7}{38}$.

Therefore, $\frac{x}{y} = \frac{-\frac{7}{38}}{\frac{4}{19}} = -\frac{7}{8}$.

39. The answer is B.

Solving for the solution set for $2 \leq 3x + 1 \leq 5$, we have

Adding -1 on all the terms → $1 \leq 3x \leq 4$

Dividing all the terms by 3 → $\frac{1}{3} \leq x \leq \frac{4}{3}$

The solution set is one infinite line segment between $\frac{1}{3}$ and $\frac{4}{3}$, inclusive.

40. The answer is A.

The number of points that Cesar can get from answering m "True or False" questions correctly would be $3m$. The number of points that Cesar can get from answering n "Multiple Choice" questions correctly would be $2n$.

To advance to the next level, Cesar needs to get at least 80 points. This means Cesar needs to get a total of 80 points or higher from answering the two types of questions.

Therefore, the inequality that can represent the problem would be $3m + 2n \geq 80$.

41. The answer is D.

Line k passes through the points (1,0) and (0,3). This means the slope of line k is -3.

The line perpendicular to line k will have a slope that is the negative of the reciprocal of the slope of line k, or have a slope of $\frac{1}{3}$.

42. The answer is C.

75% of the data will fall within 2 standard deviations of the mean.

1,500,000 + 2(75,000) = 1,650,000

1,500,000 – 2(75,000) = 1,350,000

Hence, at least 75% of all homes sold in the area will have a price range from $1,350 to $1,650,000

43. The answer is A.

We're looking for P_0.

r = 0.04 (4%)

k = 4 (4 quarters in 1 year)
N = 18
P_{18} = \$20,000

In this case, we're going to have to set up the equation, and solve for P_0.

$$20{,}000 = P_0\left(1 + \frac{0.04}{4}\right)^{18*4}$$

20,000 = P_0(2.0471)

$P_0 = \frac{20{,}000}{2.0471}$

P_0 = \$9,769.92

So you would need to deposit \$9,769.92 now to have \$40,000 in 18 years.

44. The answer is B.

The midrange is defined as the sum of the lowest and highest values in the data set divided by 2.

$$Mid\ Range = \frac{8.0 - 5.4}{2} = 1.3$$

45. The answer is C.

Total number of meters run each day= (10)(75) = 750 meters
Total number of meters run in 15 days= (750)(15) = 11,250 meters

Conversion factor: 1 kilometer = 1,000 meters

Number of kilometers in 15 days = $\frac{11{,}250}{1{,}000}$ = 11.25 kilometers

46. The answer is D.

This question is going to require some estimation and logic. First, we know that $\sqrt{25} = 5$.

Next, we know that 25 is between $2^3 = 8$ and $3^3 = 27$. Thus, $\sqrt[3]{25}$ must be between 2 and 3.

Lastly, $\sqrt[4]{25} = \sqrt{5} > \sqrt{4} = 2$.

So, $R = \sqrt{25} + \sqrt[3]{25} + \sqrt[4]{25}$ = 5 + {number between 2 and 3} + {number greater than 2} > 9.

47. The answer is D.

$r = (\frac{A}{P})^{1/t} - 1$ where A = \$11,220.41, P = \$8,000, t = 5

$r = (\frac{11,220.41}{8,000})^{0.2} - 1 = (1.4)^{0.2} - 1 = 1.07 - 1 = 0.07$

r = 7.0%

48. The answer is A.

$(x - 3)(x - 5)(x^2 - 4) = (x^2 - 8x + 15)(x^2 - 4)$
$y = x^4 - 4x^2 - 8x^3 + 32x + 15x^2 - 60$
$y = x^4 - 8x^3 + 11x^2 + 32x - 60$

49. The answer is D.

The roots of the polynomial $x^4 + 2x^3 - 9x^2 - 2x + 8 = 0$ are $x = -4, -1, 1, 2$.
Hence, the difference between the biggest and smallest root is $2 - (-4) = 2 + 4 = 6$.

50. The answer is B.

The problem says that the patch of grass doubles in size every day, which means that on any day, the patch was half the size the day before. So if the patch covers the entire field on the 48th day, it means the patch of grass was half the size of the field on the 47th day.

51. The answer is: 143

The total number of parts is 3 + 7 + 11, that is, 21.
Hence 21 parts correspond to 273 feet
1 part corresponds to $\frac{273}{21}$ = 13 feet
3 parts correspond to 3 × 13 = 39 feet
7 parts correspond to 7 × 13 = 91 feet
11 parts correspond to 11 × 13 = 143 feet
Thus, the length of the longest piece is 143 feet.

52. The answer is: 2.4

The more the number of workers, the faster the job is done. Hence, this is an inverse proportion.
3 workers can complete the task in 4 days.
1 worker takes three times as long, that is, 4 × 3 = 12 days.
5 workers can do it in one fifth of the time that one worker takes, that is, $\frac{12}{5}$ days or 2.4 days.

53. The answer is: 2.24

By direct proportion:

100% corresponds to 3.74 kg

1% corresponds to $\frac{3.74}{100}$ = 0.0374 kg

60% corresponds to 60 × 0.0374 = 2.244 kg

25% corresponds to 25 × 0.0374 = 0.935 kg

15% corresponds to 15 × 0.0374 = 0.561 kg

Thus, the masses of the copper is 2.24 kg

54. The answer is: 1.4

The sum of the first 7 terms is 35 and the common difference is 1.2.
Thus, S_7 = 35, n=7 and d =1.2.
Since the sum of n terms of an arithmetic progression is given by $S_n = \frac{n}{2}[2a_1 + (n - 1)]d$

So, then $35 = \frac{7}{2}[2a_1 + (7 - 1)1.2] = \frac{7}{2}[2a_1 + 7.2]$

Hence, $\frac{35\times2}{7} = 2a_1 + 7.2 \rightarrow 10 = 2a_1 + 7.2 \rightarrow a_1 = 1.4$.

55. The answer is: 41

$(4 - 5i)(4 + 5i) = 16 + 20i - 20i - 25i^2$ the middle terms cancel out
$= 16 - 25\,(-1)$ since $i^2 = -1$
$= 41$

56. The answer is: 7

First, think about what you have (18.5 in on the map and a scale) and what you want to know (how many miles 18.5 inches represents on the ground). It may help to think about inches on the map and inches on the ground as different units.

$18.5\ inches \text{ on the map } (\frac{24{,}000\ in \text{ on the ground}}{1\ in \text{ on the map}}) = 444{,}000\ inches \text{ on the ground}$

1 foot = 12 inches

1 mile = 5,280 feet

$444{,}000\ inches(\frac{1\ feet}{12\ inches})(\frac{1\ miles}{5{,}280\ feet}) = 7.0\ miles$

57. The answer is: 52.5

After 1 year, the bank adds 5 percent of your original 50 dollars to your account.
You then have 50 + .05(50) = (50) (1+. 05) =50(1.05) = \$52.50.

58. The answer is: 34

If we let h be the height of the electric post and d be the distance from the base of the electric post, then we have $\tan 23° = \frac{h}{d}$.

This means h = $\tan 23° \times d = \tan 23° \times 80$ = 80(0.4245) = 34 meters

53891912R00150

Made in the USA
Lexington, KY
24 July 2016